The Psalms Resculpted
A Poetic Translation

Milton L. Watt, Ph.D.

First Edition
USA

Copyright ©2025 Milton L. Watt

All rights reserved.

ISBN: 979-8-9985875-0-4

Published by Milton L. Watt
resculptingfeedback@gmail.com
April 18, 2025

Book cover design by Grace Hutchins of Inuendos Design
Co., Siloam Springs, Arkansas   www.inuendos.biz

Dedicated to my wife Linda and to my children Alicia (Baké) and John. Special thanks to Linda for her patience with me through many years of late-night work on this project.

Acknowledgements

I thank Dr. Ernst Wendland for writing the Foreword to this book, for his inspiring articles and books about translating Hebrew poetry, and for providing valuable insights as the main reader for my dissertation at Stellenbosch University.

I thank Dr. Christo van der Merwe for directing my dissertation work at Stellenbosch University and for all his helpful guidance.

I thank Dr. Lynell Zogbo for her teaching and writing about translating Hebrew poetry and allowing me to co-lead with her a beautiful Hebrew poetry workshop in Niger for the Fulani translation teams of the Sahel region of Africa.

I thank Dr. Brenda Boerger for her valuable insights and support during the writing process.

I thank Dr. Sebastian Floor for his vision of bringing the Psalms to all languages of the world using contextualized rhythms, instruments, dance, and words through the Psalms that Sing project and for the privilege of being part of this work.

Foreword by Dr. Ernst Wendland

In this new translation of the biblical Psalter, experienced translation consultant, teacher, and trainer, Dr. Milton Watt, applies a rarely applied approach to the task—namely, providing an English rendering that seeks to duplicate something of the poetic sound of the original Hebrew text. He adopts a new term to metaphorically describe his methodology—"resculpting." In his PhD thesis, this is defined as "a moderately restructured and meaning-based translation of a poetic sacred text based on theological, thematic, and other literary/rhetorical concerns" (iii).

In his modern rendition, Dr. Watt seeks to retain certain important aspects of the biblical text, for example:

- above all and most comprehensively, its essential semantic meaning, although at times this is redistributed textually in the English version;
- to a great extent, the prominent poetic formal feature of lined parallelism;
- for the most part, the original versification, which is occasionally modified to allow for the reorganization of meaning noted above.

So what has been modified, or "resculpted," in order to lyricize this version for an attentive English-speaking audience and readership? The following is a selection of the devices employed by this contemporary poet-translator to highlight the "melody" of the spoken word—to give it more "life":

- The primary feature of this new translation is twofold and immediately apparent, namely, the use of end-rhyme and frequently also syllabic rhythm, as illustrated in the example below.
- Visually, the printed text is formatted in two important ways to display crucial features of the original discourse arrangement—its strophic (poetic paragraph) structure and the development of related thought patterns through paralleled line indentations.
- While natural spoken English is generally used, at times unusual lexical combinations or syntactic structures, e.g., word order, are employed to highlight some poetic feature of the Hebrew text.

- The translation is literarily "contextualized" periodically in the interest of greater communicability through the use of idiomatic language and terminology, but instances of transculturation and anachronism are avoided.
- Footnotes are employed in order to explain certain important linguistic or literary aspects of the Hebrew text or to comment on the use of implied information in the English version.
- Several prominent, sometimes controversial technical features of the Psalms are either included in the translation (e.g., the superscriptions in *italics*) or marginally noted (e.g., the Hebrew letters for the acrostic psalms).

For whom is this resculpted version of the Psalter intended? Dr. Watt states that he designed this creative translation "to be meditated upon for personal reflection or to be read from the pulpit" (p. 1) during services of public worship. I might add several other potential uses: as an auxiliary text for a congregational Bible study or an academic course on the Psalms; as another reference version for Bible translators seeking to produce a more poetic rendering of the Psalter in their language; and possible also as the base text for English-speaking choirs around the world who wish to compose a more musical version of a selected psalm.

The proverb, "Proof of the pudding is in the eating," dates back centuries to usage in Middle English, but its truth is relevant to many situations yet today, including *The Psalms Resculpted.* How do they "taste" to you (sound, instruct, inspire) as you read the following short, but well-known sample? I'm sure that you'll be "refreshed" in more ways than one.

Psalm 23:1-3 (p. 33)

A psalm written by David.

1 The LORD's my shepherd,[28]
    my shepherd is he.[29]
For all of my needs
    he takes care of me.
2 In fresh green pastures
    he makes me to lie.
Beside hushed waters
    he leads me right by.
3 My soul is restored,
    refreshed from on high.[30]
Along righteous paths[31]
    he guides me along
to honor his name
    to keep me from wrong.[32]

---

28 Every line in the poem is five syllables. This is an attempt to translate the simplicity and succinctness of David's compact original poem.

29 This repetition is added for rhythmic and poetic purposes.

30 This detail is not part of the Hebrew text. It is certainly implied that his refreshment is coming from the LORD.

31 This could be a physical image like "right paths" or the more spiritual "righteous paths". The Hebrew text is ambiguous and perhaps means both.

32 This line is implied but not in the Hebrew text.

Psalm 45:1 (p. 63)

My thoughts overflow
with words apropos.
    My tongue is the pen
    that writes like wise men.
      My verses I'll sing
      as I speak to the king.

Prof. Ernst R. Wendland
Stellenbosch University, Ancient Studies
Dallas International University, Applied Linguistics

Introduction

Overview
This work is a poetic translation of the Psalms into English. It aims to communicate the faithful meaning of the original Hebrew text and to capture the emotion of the Psalms. It pays attention to how the message sounds, because poetry is more than a meaningful message, it is beautiful language.

It is designed to be meditated upon for personal reflection but can be read from the pulpit. It is written with a sensitivity toward a Jewish audience but reflecting my Christian bias towards a New Testament fulfillment of many messianic Psalms through Christ. I created this translation from a background as a Bible translator, Bible translation consultant, Hebrew poetry specialist, and poet.

No translation is perfect. 150 artistic creations which communicate *faithfully* the biblical message present a supreme challenge. Many details can be improved. So, I give opportunity for feedback at the end of this Introduction.

Methodology
I am applying my own technique to create this Psalms version.

Resculpting
My technique follows in the footsteps of what is more technically called a Literary Functional Equivalent translation (Ernst Wendland's term "LiFE translation"). It aims to be a faithful translation of the original text.

My translation approach is a term that I coined called "resculpting." This methodology stems from my 2015 Stellenbosch University Ph.D. dissertation on the topic entitled, *Re-sculpting a Sacred Text: Towards an Acceptable Poetic Translation of the Psalms – Exemplified by Psalms 131 and 150* This is freely downloadable at: http://sun.academia.edu/EWENDLAND/Dissertations. After clicking, go to the search bar and type "Psalms 131 and 150" and you will find the PDF document.

1

The major goals of my resculpting translation are to keep as close as possible to the meaning of the Hebrew and to create a poetic message in English using a "rhyming organizational principle." These two goals are in constant tension and to accomplish this aim one must change the form of the original text into recognizable poetic forms in English and attempt to preserve the meaning in the process.

Here is a brief resculpted example of the refrain in Psalm 8:1,9:

YOU WHO MADE US, O LORD, OUR LORD.
HOW MIGHTY YOUR NAME IN THIS WIDE WORLD!

Summary of My Approach

I always try to keep the **shape** of the original text. The shape of the original message itself is important, and I believe it must be preserved in translation. This means that there is no radical restructuring of the whole psalm as a "re-creation" methodology would do. There is an occasional combining of verses, but generally not more than three or four verses. In most cases I keep the biblical verse-by-verse order but will sometimes move information within the verse. This approach gives me **flexibility** to find poetic forms suitable for English poetry.

Natural and Unnatural
Changing form from one language to another is a basic principle of creating a natural translation which is my overall goal. I seek to understand the meaning of the original text and then transfer that meaning to the target (translated) text. But sometimes I translate unnaturally to grab attention or accentuate something. Poets break the rules of grammar for reflective purposes. It is all a difficult process to explain because you always "lose" something when you translate, and you can be accused of distorting or betraying the original text (*traduttore traditore* "to translate is to betray"). It is an art and a science.

Rhyme and Free Verse
My overall poetic technique is to use end rhymes, typically on alternate even lines, but occasionally there will be rhymes on consecutive lines, double rhymes (odd and even lines), or other rhyme patterns including rhymes within the same line (intraline). Sometimes I use near rhymes.

Rhyme in English was once very popular between the 12th and 20th centuries and is still popular in modern English songs, Spoken word poetry, and Rap (often extreme rhyme). It is less popular in modern poetry circles in general because free verse is the preferred mode of expression among modern poets. But the Psalms were originally **songs** in Hebrew, and **rhyme** is the favored structure of contemporary English songs. Therefore, I feel that rhyme is the closest structural **match** to a song in biblical Hebrew, even though Hebrew only rarely uses rhyme. I have occasionally used refrains since they are popular in English songs, but I mostly use them where there is a likely refrain in the Hebrew text.

Rhythm and Melody
I have used a variety of rhyming and rhythmic techniques. I have sometimes used free verse (typically non-rhyme). The structure or rhythm chosen is intended to try to capture the mood of the psalm as I sense it poetically. A few poems are a mix of rhyming and non-rhyming styles like Psalm 22. Since I am striving for smoothness and rhythm in English, I also use quite a few contractions (I'm, you're, etc.) which is not typical in most traditional English translations of the Psalms.

I have not attempted to suggest a melody for my poetic versions of the psalms. However, I am sure that they could easily be created for each psalm. But the poetic text itself can be appreciated without a melody.

Accuracy and Footnotes
My text has been checked against the Hebrew text, but I referred to dozens of translations and many commentaries for ideas. It is not a concordant translation – some terms may be translated in different ways for poetic effect – but there is a general consistency, including superscriptions.

I have used footnotes for major technical comments that needed to be made, but I have tried to keep them to a minimum. I have not generally footnoted small changes to the Hebrew text that involve slight changes to make the text poetic, but I've tried to footnote larger added information to the text. Often adjustments are necessary to beautify the text to become a poetic English style.

I strive not to twist the meaning of the text by adding too much interpretive content. If content is added, it is for rhyme, beauty, etc. I tried to footnote many of the major changes where my text differs from the Hebrew Masoretic text. Anything added would also be biblically sound and taught elsewhere in Scripture, but I normally try to find implied information from the context that does not add or take away from the text. In several tightly structured poems (example, Psalms 25, 66, and 119) I use more latitude in creating the psalm to produce a highly rhythmic and rhyming effect through double rhyme.

Contextualized but Not Anachronistic

I try not to transculturate the text. This means that I try not to change the cultural context of the original message. The Psalms were written by Jewish poets for principally a Jewish audience thousands of years ago. It would not be a true *translation* in my view if it is anachronistic. For example, I would not want to use terms like nuclear bombs, radio, television, and movies, nor would it contain a New Testament cultural perspective. The message is contextualized to a certain extent with modern idioms, terms, and modern parallels for the purpose of communicating and engaging interest without being anachronistic.

Technical Terms

Yahweh is usually translated as "the LORD," but sometimes as "Yahweh" or "GOD" (like the Message) for poetic or stylistic reasons. Similarly, *Yah* is usually translated as "the LORD." But *hallelu-Yah* has been translated "Hallelu-Yah, praise the LORD." In some cases, a line has been added like "Let praise to him be outpoured" or something similar for poetic effect.

Adonai is translated as "the Lord." The special name *Adonai Yahweh* is translated as "my Lord Yahweh" and *Yahweh Adonai* is translated as "Yahweh, my Lord." *Yahweh Elohai* is translated as "my LORD God" or "LORD my God". *Yahweh Tseba'ot* is translated as "the LORD God Almighty," "the LORD of all," or "the LORD who rules over all," and sometimes it is footnoted.

Selah is translated as Dr. Murray Salisbury recommends: "Pause and Reflect" which some scholars think could derive from the etymology of *selah* "lift up," but this meaning is simply an educated guess. *Selah* most likely means a reflective pause or musical interlude.

Acrostics and Superscriptions
Seven of the Psalms (25, 34, 37, 111, 112, 119, 145) are acrostic psalms.
They follow verse-by-verse the order of the Hebrew alphabet. The first
verse starts with a word that begins with *aleph*, the second with *beth*, etc.
In the acrostic psalms the Hebrew letter itself is shown plus its
transliteration into English, but there is no attempt to try to imitate the
acrostic equivalent into English which could make the text less natural.

I believe that the superscriptions of the Psalms are basically accurate,
helpful and give a context to many of the Psalms, so I have preserved them
in italics at the top of the psalm where they occur. Superscriptions are part
of the Hebrew text itself in the Hebrew manuscripts we have available.
This means that superscriptions were added very early on in the process of
copying texts, but we do not know the historical details.

I interpret the term in the superscriptions *le dawid* "to David" to mean
authorship, that is, "written by David." I believe that David wrote about
half of the Psalms, maybe more. Similarly, "written by the descendants of
Korah" (Psalm 48), "written by Moses" (Psalm 90), "written by Solomon"
(Psalms 72, 127).

Background of the Psalms
Although they are passed down to us in written form as songs, we have no
record of how they sounded and only a few details of how they were used
in corporate worship. 1 Chronicles 16 records large excerpts of Psalms 96,
105, and 106 (with small differences), sung when David brought the ark to
Jerusalem. The songs were performed with instruments and choirs.

Background of the Author
Milton Watt received an M.A. in Missions/Cross-Cultural Studies from
Wheaton Graduate School, an M.Div, Th.M. from Trinity International
University in Deerfield Illinois and a Ph.D. in Biblical Studies from
Stellenbosch University, South Africa. He is a Bible translation consultant
with SIM who works under Seed Company's **administration**. He lived and
worked in West Africa for 20 years, training a Bible translation team and
helping to complete a New Testament in 2018. He's worked with dozens
of teams as a translation consultant over the past 20 years, specializing
now in the Psalms and the Psalms that Sing project.

5

Larger Sample of "The Psalms Resculpted"

Psalm 13:1-4

For the music director. A psalm written by David.

1-2 O LORD, how long will this go on?
    Please remember me!
You're a million miles away right now.
    When will you set me free?
Raging waves of anguish besiege me.
    I'm crushed with sorrow each day.
How long will my foes prevail over me,
    succeeding in their way?

3 Answer me, O my God!
    I'm at the end of my rope.
I'm on the verge of death.
    Give me light, LORD, give me hope!
        4 Lest my foes say they've won it all,
        or be jubilant when I fall.

Psalm 137:1-4

1 There at the rivers of Babylon,
when we thought about Jerusalem,
    we hung our heads and cried.
2 On the willows there, we hung up our harps,
3 when our captors tortured us with barbs.
    We felt like we had died.[1]
They asked for joyful songs, short or long.[2]
"Hey, sing for us a Zion song!"
    they made as a demand.
4 But how can we strike up singing,
the LORD's choruses ringing
    in a foreign land?

---

[1] This line is implied but not part of the Hebrew text.
[2] "Short or long" is not part of the Hebrew text.

Psalm 119:9-12
ב (Beth)
9 If young people live in step with your word,
      they'll stay pure through all life's demands.
10 I'll seek you with a heart all stirred,
      let me not leave your commands.
11 I've hidden your promises inward,
      so I won't sin against you.
12 I praise you, please teach me, O LORD,
      all your demands so true.

Psalm 19:1-6
For the music director. A psalm written by David.

1 The marvelous, well-crafted heavens
      declare the glory of God.
2-4 Night after night,
      day after day,
without word or sound,
      their silence speaks
          holds sway ...
      reaching, preaching
         to the whole world
            proclaiming him each day.
In the midst of heaven's canvas
      there lies the sun –
5 dashing bridegroom
      happy hero ...
         its measured course to run.
6 Traversing sky.
      None can hide from
      its heat so fierce ...
         once its journey's begun.

Abbreviations

The footnotes contain the following standard abbreviations:

ANE – Ancient Near East
ex – Example
lit – Literally
NT – New Testament
Ps – Psalm
Pss – Psalms
trad – Traditionally
v – Verse
vv – Verses

The footnotes also refer to the following Biblical versions:

CEV – Contemporary English Version
CSB – Christian Standard Bible
ERV – Easy-to-Read Version
ESV – English Standard Version
GNB – Good News Bible
NCV – New Century Version
NET – New English Translation (called the NET Bible)
NIV – New International Version (2011, if not specified as below)
    NIV84 – New International Version (1984)
    NIV11 – New International Version (2011)
NKJV – New King James Version
NLT – New Living Translation
NRSV – New Revised Standard
RSV – Revised Standard Version

Feedback

I welcome all feedback. I plan to keep track of any feedback that I receive. If I receive enough feedback, I plan to revise this edition in the near future. Please contact me at resculptingfeedback@gmail.com for any correspondence.

Milton L. Watt, Ph.D.
Feb 19, 2026

> *Enter his presence with singing.*
> *Serve him with glad hearts ringing.* (Ps 100:2ab)

Book 1 (Psalms 1-41)

Psalm 1

[1] Favored is the one, that one,[3]...
>   not marching to the wicked's beat,
>   nor standing on the sinner's street,
>   nor sitting in the scoffer's seat.
>> [2] Instead this one has pure delight
>> in probing GOD's word[4] day and night,
>> absorbing it to gain insight.
>   [3] This one will be just like a tree.
>   Each season precious fruit you'll see.
>   In all that's done – prosperity.
>> How full and verdant – its leaves and shoots,
>> for near a stream are fixed its roots.
>> By the stream comes forth good fruits.

[4] Contrastively are wicked shown
to be like chaff that wind has blown,
like chaff that wind has blown.
>   [5] When judgment day is full at hand,
>   the wicked ones, they will not stand –
>   no, not with the righteous band.

[6] Yes, GOD guides well the pure one's path.
The wicked's way just leads to wrath –
a fatal path that leads to wrath.

---

[3] The Hebrew text shows a singular "one" in contrast to the plural "wicked ones," "sinners," and "scoffers" of the next three lines. This contrast is made clear in Ps 1 by the "one" mentioned several times throughout the poem. In v 1 "the wicked," "the sinner," and "the scoffer" are to be understood generically as plurals.

[4] The "word" is *Torah* in Hebrew. *Torah* means "teaching" or "instruction" and that is the usual translation in "Psalms Resculpted." It still has that general meaning here, but "word" was chosen for rhythmic considerations. I interpret *Torah* here with the force of "all of God's word/teaching/instruction." Yet, for a Jew it seems there is often some association to the narrower meaning of the law as given through Moses.

Psalm 2

1-2 Plotting and churning,
    nations in an uproar ...
        so futile.
    Raging and fuming
        against him on high ...
        why?
                Earth's rulers, thinking to be wise
                rise up as one and strategize ...
                    against the LORD
                    against his choice,5
        3 they cry:
                "Let's break the chains of these 'lords.'
                Let's loosen their binding cords."

4-5 But on high ...
    the lofty Exalted One, the Lord,
    laughs and mocks at them,
        rebukes, ... terrifies,
        and in hot anger ... replies:
                6 "On my holy hill, Mount Zion,
                I've placed my choice, my Royal One."

7 Then this King testifies:
    "I will speak forth the LORD's decree:
    'You are my Son,' he said to me,
    'This day your Father I will be.
        8 Ask me for a possession.
            I'll give you to earth's corners:
        nation on nation.
                9 With an iron rod you'll dash them!
                Like a potter's pot you'll smash them!'"

10 So now, O kings, O magistrates,
be warned and think about your fates.

---

5 Lit. "his anointed," which is a reference to the Messiah. Even many Jewish scholars view this as a messianic psalm.

¹¹ Serve the LORD with reverence now.
Rejoice and tremble as you bow.
¹² Worship the Pure One⁶ lest GOD's ire rise,
and you perish in the way,
for his anger flares up quickly,
but those in him: favored are they!

Psalm 3

A psalm written by David when he fled from his son Absalom.

¹ O LORD, my foes are so many
who've risen up against me.
² This nay-saying crowd is saying:
"No help from God will he see."⁷ *Pause and reflect*

³ But you, O LORD, bring me honor.
You lift up my head, help me win.
You are my shield, my protection.
You're with me through thick and thin.
⁴ I lifted my voice before him,
to the LORD intensely I cried.
My words were not arrows amiss.⁸
From his holy hill he replied.   *Pause and reflect*

⁵ I laid down, I slept, then awoke,
for he's my LORD, my protection.
⁶ I won't fear ten thousand people
who plot against me insurrection.

---

⁶ Trad. "Kiss the Son." In the ANE, kissing the feet of the king was a sign of submission to his rule and authority. The Hebrew word *bar* can mean "Pure One." I understand "Pure One" to refer back to "my Son" in v 7, "my Royal One" (my King) in v 6, and "his choice" (anointed one) in vv 1-2. See Academia article by Anne Garber Kompaore *Understanding BAR in Psalm 2:12*. More holistically, the "Pure One" in v 12 alludes back to the "anointed" (his choice) in vv 1-2 to complete the Psalm with the effect of an inclusio (God and his Son working together against the leaders of the world who oppose them).
⁷ The word *Selah* is used here for the first time in the book of Psalms. See the Introduction for why I interpret this as "Pause and reflect."
⁸ The image of "arrows" is not in the Hebrew text, but it communicates the general idea of the psalmist with a powerful metaphor, relevant to the context.

11

7 Now you, my LORD God, rise up!
     May deliverance come from your hand.
Shatter the teeth of the wicked.
     Strike jaws in the enemy's camp!
8 The LORD is he who delivers.
     Oh, bless your people again!   *Pause and reflect*

Psalm 4

For the music director. A psalm written by David, to be accompanied
with stringed instruments.

1 O God, you're right in all you do,
so answer when I call to you.
     Relieve this anguish I bear.
     Be gracious now, hear my prayer.

2 O people, how long will you mock me?
     And shame me, too, ... for how long?
How long will you love what is worthless?
     How long will you seek after wrong? *Pause and reflect*
3 Of this you can be certain,
     O people, one and all:
The LORD himself keeps the faithful.
     He'll answer when I call.

4 In anger,9 O people, don't sin.
     Be silent, reflect in night's hush.   *Pause and reflect*
5 With pure hearts do sacrifices.
     In the LORD put all your trust.

6 There are many around me who say:
     "Who'll show us a ray of hope?"
 May the glow of your glorious face, LORD,
     shine on us and help us to cope.
7 You have gladdened my heart so much more than
their harvests of grain and new wine can.
          8 I will lie down in peace and sleep.
          Only you, LORD, my safety can keep.

---

9 This interpretation is based on the Septuagint.

Psalm 5

For the music director. A psalm written by David,
to be accompanied with flutes.

1-2 LORD, hear my groans and the words I pray.
Give ear, my King, and help me today.
>3 As morning breaks, my voice you hear.
As morning marches, I draw near.
I watch, wait, anticipate
your response as I persevere.[10]

4 You detest wickedness, O God,
no evil dwells in you.
5 In your sight no boasters stand.
You hate all the wrong they do.
6 You abhor and destroy liars,
and all who murder too.

7 Lavishing your loyal love on me,
I draw near with fear and awe.
I'll bow down toward your temple ...
so holy, without flaw.
8 Make clear the way before me,
for my enemies bring me strife.
Lead me, O LORD, in upright paths
to live holy throughout my life.[11]

9 With their mouths, my foes speak lies:
Their stomachs: pits of destruction.
Their throats: graves open wide.
Their tongues: webs of seduction.
10 O God, hold them not guiltless.
By their own plots let them fall.
Cast them out for sins multiplied.
They're like rebels seeking a brawl!

---

[10] David is persevering in prayer. He is waiting expectantly in the Lord's presence for an answer to his request, keeping vigil like a watchman.
[11] This last line of v 8 is implied, and it brings out the line "lead me in your righteousness."

¹¹ Protect those who seek your protection.
>May they ever rejoice in you.
May all those who love you adoringly
>exult in your name so true.
¹² You shield the just with your favor, O LORD.
>You bless them in all they do.

Psalm 6

For the music director. A psalm written by David, to be accompanied
with an eight-stringed instrument and other stringed instruments.

¹⁻² O LORD,
>my bones tremble, ... panic nears, ...
>gnawing numbness, weakness, fears. ...
Heal me, save me,
>I need your grace.
Don't chasten me in anger.
>With favor turn your face.
³ O LORD,
>my soul trembles ... panic nears.
>How long? How long? Ease my fears.
⁴ Turn to me, help me.
>I need your might.
Because of your loyal love,
>save me from my plight.
>>⁵ For who remembers you in death?
>>There's no praise where there's no breath!

⁶ My groaning seems unending,
>weighs on me, wears me out.
Sorrow is my night-long mate,
>and tears flood my couch.
⁷ Because of all who hate me,
>my spent eyes melt away.
Distress blurs my vision
>all throughout the day.

⁸ O evil ones, go away,
    the LORD's heard my weeping.
⁹ He has heard my urgent pleas –
    his promises keeping.¹²
¹⁰ May my rivals turn back in shock.
    May they quickly leave in shame.
May my foes be fully thwarted,
    who seek to soil my name.¹³

Psalm 7

A dramatic¹⁴ song written by David which he sang to the LORD about Cush, from the tribe of Benjamin.

¹⁻² Hunting me, pursuing me like lions,
    my flesh they seek to devour.
They hope to drag me and maul me to bits
    by their mighty power.
O LORD, my God in whom I hide,
    save me at this dark hour.

³ O LORD, if my hands have done wrong
    or I've strayed from your laws,
⁴ if I've betrayed a friend lifelong
    or harmed my foe without cause,
⁵ then let my rival entrap me,
    let him dash me to the ground.
Let him come and overwhelm me,
    so my life can't be found.   *Pause and reflect*

---

¹² David is sure that God "has heard his weeping" so I added the implied notion that this assurance is based on his promises that he hears our prayers, though this is not clearly stated in the text.
¹³ This last line of the song is implied.
¹⁴ This is the interpretation of a rare expression in Hebrew. One interpretation is that it reflects the idea of a dramatic movement in the pitch of the song (high and low notes) or it could be how the song is presented (for example, its tune or musical arrangement).

⁶ Just Judge of all, come to my side.
  Lᴏʀᴅ God in your ire, arise
against my furious foes,
  and their fomenting cries.
⁷ From your highly exalted view,
  as you sit above and look down.
Nations are surrounding you,
  peoples are gathered around.
⁸ You judge all the peoples, ... and me.
Let them see my integrity.
  O Most High, I've done no wrong.
  I've been blameless all along.
⁹ May the wicked's evil be through,
but establish those who are true.
  The thoughts and desires you test,
  O God of righteousness.
¹⁰⁻¹¹ You burn against the wicked each day,
O Judge, righteous in every way.
  For me you're a shield and rampart,
  saving the noble of heart.

¹² If a person will not repent,
  God will clean and sharpen his sword,
He'll take his bowstring, pulling it bent,
  ready to strike at his word.
   ¹³ He makes fiery arrows with skill.
   He prepares war weapons that kill.

¹⁴ Sower of evil
reaps upheaval.
  ¹⁵ Digger of pit
  falls into it.
   ¹⁶ The violence he led
   falls back on his head.

[17] Because God is righteous,
　　my thanks I'll proclaim.
To the LORD Most High,
　　I'll sing praise to his name.

Psalm 8

For the music director. A psalm accompanied by the harp used at Gath.
Written by David.

[1] YOU WHO MADE US, O LORD, OUR LORD.
HOW MIGHTY YOUR NAME IN THIS WIDE WORLD!

Your glory, it lies
far above the skies!
　　[2] In the seemingly mundane,
　　　　you've ordained that praise should flow.
　　From the mouths of little children,
　　　　you've silenced the raging foe.

[3] As I gaze upon your night sky –
　　your great artwork: each moon and star,
[4] why is it you care about us mortals,
　　and visit us from afar?
[5] You've made us a bit lower than yourself,[15]
　　and glorified these clay jars.

[6] Over your handiwork
　　you say: "Oversee!"
You tell us to rule,
　　with authority:
　　　　[7] O'er tame and wild beasts,
　　　　　　[8] o'er birds of air, fish of sea,
　　o'er all that weave their way
　　　　through waves so free.

[9] YOU WHO MADE US, O LORD, OUR LORD.
HOW MIGHTY YOUR NAME IN THIS WIDE WORLD!

---

[15] This could also be translated as "God," "gods," "angels," or "divine beings."
The Septuagint translates this as "angels" and that is what is quoted in the NT. "A
bit lower" is to emphasize mankind's position between God and his creatures.

17

Psalm 9

For the music director. To be sung to the tune "The Death of the Son."
A psalm written by David.

¹ I thank you O LORD with my whole heart.
  All your wonders I'll proclaim.
² O God Most High, I'll exult in you,
  singing praises to your name.
³ My foes are destroyed by your power.
  They stumble, turn back in despair.
⁴ You've vindicated my case for me,
  enthroned as a judge who's fair.
⁵ You've killed the wicked, rebuked the nations,
  erased for all times their names.
⁶ You've ruined my foes, uprooted their towns,
  destroyed the mere thought of their fame.

⁷ But the LORD sits as king forever.
  On his throne he judges justly.
⁸ He judges the nations with fairness,
  and rules the world righteously.
⁹ The LORD is a shelter for crushed ones,
  a refuge in dark stormy days.
¹⁰ He's faithful to those who seek him,
  who know him and trust his ways.

¹¹ Praise the LORD who lives in Zion, yes sing!
  Proclaim his deeds to the nations.
¹² He avenges blood spilled, and won't forget cries
  from poor people's situations.
¹³ Have mercy, LORD, my foes oppress me.
  Lift me up as I near the grave,
¹⁴ that I may tell your praises in Zion
  and be joyful in how you save.

15-16 The LORD is known by his justice,
     the wicked self-destruct, cannot stand.
The nations have sunk into pits they've made,
     their lives caught in traps they've planned.
               Meditation, Pause and reflect

17 The wicked and all godless nations,
     together go down to the pit.
18 But God won't forget the oppressed.
     Their hope flame will always be lit.

19 Rise up, LORD, let man not prevail!
     May the nations be judged before you.
20 Cause them great dread, O LORD, assail!
     Mere humans, from your high view.   *Pause and reflect*

Psalm 10
               (continued)[16]

1 LORD, why do you stand at a distance,
     and hide in troubled times,
2 while wicked ones track down the poor
     with prideful plots and crimes?

3-4 The wicked and greedy are boastful.
     They follow their own lustful dreams.
Out of pride they hate and won't seek the LORD.
     There's no room for him in their schemes.
5 They dismiss all his laws, scoff at their foes,
     yet prosper in all of their ways.
6 They say they won't change, and no harm will come,
     to them or their seed all their days.

---

[16] Many scholars think that Pss 9 and 10 were one psalm in the past because there is evidence of a broken acrostic linking both psalms. Most scholars argue that anywhere from 5 to 7 letters of the 22-letter Hebrew alphabet are missing. It seems that they were later divided into two psalms. It is helpful to view Pss 9 and 10 together, looking at the expressions, themes, and artistry.

7 Deceit and lies, curses and threats,
  all of these roll off each tongue.
8 They stealthily wait near the small towns,
  and from there an ambush is sprung.
They secretly watch for their victims,
  9 like lions catching prey unawares.
They covertly kill the guiltless,
  they seize them with nets, hooks and snares.

10 Their victims are trounced and bowed down,
  forced by their strength to bend knees.
11 They say to themselves, "God has no concern,
  he hides and never sees."

12 Rise up LORD, extend your hand to the weak.
  Don't forget the poor, don't discount.
13 Why do the wicked spurn God and say:
  "We won't be called to account"?

14 But, O God, who helps the orphans:
  The guiltless trust fully in you.
You LORD feel their trouble and grief:
  All this you see from your view.
15 Disarm the power of each wicked one,
  who thought: "We won't be discovered!".
And make them pay for the deeds they done,
  deeds they thought were well-covered.

16 The LORD is king eternally.
  The nations will cease from his land.
17 You hear the cry of the needy,
  you sustain them, stretch forth your hand.
18 You make it so that mere humans
  will no more cause terror and woe,
for you judge fairly the orphans,
  and defend each one who's brought low.

Psalm 11

For the music director. Written by David.

¹ In the LORD I find shelter,
    so how dare you tell me:
"Go now, take flight like a bird.
    Go to a mountain, flee!"
² The wicked place arrows and bend back bows.
    They have fine-tuned their art.
They pull their strings in crafty shadows
    to shoot the pure of heart.

³ When society's pillars crumble,
    what can the godly do?
4-5 The LORD sits on his holy temple throne,
    and each on earth he can view.
He tests the godly and the wicked,
    examining all they do.
But those who love to do violence,
    he hates them at levels so deep,
⁶ he'll rain heat on them: hot sulfur and coals –
    a sizzling whirlwind they'll reap.

⁷ Yes, the LORD is just, justice he'll savor.
Those doing right will find his favor.

Psalm 12

*For the music director. A psalm written by David, to be accompanied
with an eight-stringed instrument.*

¹ Help O LORD, for the godly are no more.
    The faithful vanish from the world.
² Neighbors deceive neighbors deeply with lies.
    Sweet talk from their tongue is unfurled.
3-4 The LORD will silence the prideful who say:
    "Our words, no one can curtail.
We are masters of our own destiny.
    With our tongues we will prevail."

5 But the LORD says:
    "I'll rise up for the poor and needy,
        those groaning, oppressed and in pain.
    I'll guard them from those who attack them
        and safety they will obtain."

        6 The LORD's words are pure like silver refined,
        perfectly17 pure, they can't be outshined.

7 You watch, LORD, the needy and preserve them,
    and guard them from the wicked always.
8 Yet sadly the wicked walk freely around:
    The world exalts vile with praise.

Psalm 13
        For the music director. A psalm written by David.
1-2 O LORD, how long will this go on?
    Please remember me!
You're a million miles away right now.
    When will you set me free?
Raging waves of anguish besiege me.
    I'm crushed with sorrow each day.
How long will my foes prevail over me,
    succeeding in their way?

3 Answer me, O my God!
    I'm at the end of my rope.
I'm on the verge of death.
        Give me light, LORD, give me hope!
                4 Lest my foes say they've won it all,
                or be jubilant when I fall.

5 But I trust in your loyal love.
        I rejoice that you've set me free.
6 I'll sing forth praise to you LORD,
        for you've been gracious to me.

---

17 Lit. "Seven times pure" which means absolutely pure.

Psalm 14

For the music director. Written by David.

1 The morally bankrupt thinks:
"God means nothing to me."
They are corrupt, their ways are vile.
They act abominably.
NO ONE DOES WHAT IS GOOD.

2 From heaven the LORD looks down
on the entire human race,
to see whether there are any wise,
who sincerely seek his face.
3 All are corrupt and turn – each one
NO ONE DOES GOOD ...
not even one.

4 Do these evildoers not understand?
They consume my people like bread.
They do not call on the name of the LORD,
but trust themselves instead.[18]
5 Yet they will be terrified,
for God is with those who do right.
6 Evildoers have shamed the poor,
yet the LORD protects them each night.[19]

7 Oh that out of Zion for Israel's sake
salvation would come!
When the LORD restores their lives,
they will be glad for what he's done.

Psalm 15

A psalm written by David.

1 WHO CAN LIVE WITH YOU, O LORD,
IN YOUR TENT ON YOUR HOLY HILL?[20]
2 The one who lives right and does right,
and speaks truth with no ill will.

---

[18] This line is implied and not in the Hebrew text. Line 4c is lit. "call on Yahweh."
[19] "Each night" is added to represent an implied continual protection.
[20] This leading question and its summary at the end of the poem are highlighted.

3 The one who treats others correctly,
>   whether a neighbor or friend,
not passing along gossip and rumors,
>   not seeking to offend.
4 They despise those whom God rejects,
>   but honor those fearing the LORD.
And no matter the cost or how hard,
>   they're always true to their word.
5 They lend money without any interest,
>   and against a blameless one,
they won't take a bribe to accuse him
>   for something he's not done.
WHOEVER ACTS IN THIS WAY,
WON'T BE SHAKEN, COME WHAT MAY.

Psalm 16

A special psalm written by David.

1 Guard me, O God, for I hide in you.
>   Protect me, it's you I seek out.[21]
2 My only goodness is found in you, LORD.
>   "You're my Master," I speak out.
3 The saints of the land are noble and true,
>   in them I find great delight.
4 But those who chase after worthless gods
>   will increase their sorrows outright.
Blood offerings to them I won't ever accept,
>   their names I will never recite.

5 You LORD, are my heritage, my cup.
>   My fate you hold in your hand.
6 The boundary lines of what I'll inherit
>   bring me beauty as you've planned.

---

[21] "It's you I seek out" is implied in David's plea, but it is not part of the Hebrew text.

7-8 I'll keep my eyes on the LORD always.
  I'll stand firm because of his might.
I'll praise the LORD, who guides me when troubled,
  who teaches me each night.

9 So I will rejoice with my whole being,
  and I will feel safe and sound.
10 You won't leave your just one entombed,
  nor let me decay in the ground.22
11 You reveal to me the right road of life,
  full joy in you is found.
The pleasant things of your presence,
  forever they'll abound.

Psalm 17

A prayer written by David.

1 LORD, to my just cause, hear.
To my prayer, give ear.
    Listen to my plea,
    made with honesty.
        2 May my acquittal come from you,
        for you see all that's fair and true.

3 Though you probe deeply my heart,
    though you prove me in the night,
and test me within – through and through,
    you'll find that my thoughts are right.
I've not sinned against you.
        4 Now as to cruel men and their creed,
        I've not followed their paths,
    but to your words I heed.
            5 My steps are on your track.
            I have not fallen back.

6 I ask you, God, to hear.
To my prayer, bend your ear.

---

22 This verse refers to David and to the Messiah. Christians apply this to Jesus because of the citation of this verse in Acts 2:25-28.

Listen now to my plea.
I know you'll answer me.
7 Manifest the wonders of your love,
    you who saves with your strong arm.
You rescue those who find shelter in you,
    from foes who seek to do harm.

8 Guard me as a precious one in your sight.
    Hide me in safety under your wings.
9 Protect me from foes who swarm in on me,
    who surround me with deadly slings.
10 They harden their callous uncaring hearts
    and with prideful words they bray.
11 They've followed my tracks and circle around
    to hurl me down and slay,
12 like a lion lurking and longing
    or a wolfpack hungry for prey.

13 Arise LORD, face them, make them bow down.
    With your sword save me from their strife.
14 By your power deliver me from these foes,
    whose riches are in this life.
Punish the wicked with what you've stored up,
    may their sons gorge on this treasure.
And then may their seed living after them
    have leftovers beyond measure!

15 But I, after my acquittal comes,
    I'll look upon you in your place.
When I wake up, I'll be filled to the full,
    by seeing you face to face.

Psalm 18

For the music director. Written by David, the servant of the LORD. He sang the words of this song to the LORD when the LORD had rescued him from the power of all his enemies and from Saul's power. He said:

1 O LORD, I love you.
You're my strength through and through.

² O Rock, my Fortress, my Safe place, my God,
    my Hiding place in cliffs of power,
like a bull's strong horn who rescues me,
    my Shield and my High tower.
³ I called on you Lord who deserves all praise.
    You've crushed all my foes to this hour!
⁴⁻⁵ Face to face with the snares of death,
    the Grave's firm clutches strangled me.
Floods of worthless men upon me raged,
    and Death's dark cords entangled me.
⁶ In deep distress I cried for help.
    To the Lord God my cry rang out.
He heard me from his holy house.
    Before him my words sang out.

⁷ Suddenly: quivering and quaking:
    The earth greatly trembled and roared.
The bases of mountains were shaking
    from the anger of the Lord.

⁸ From his mouth blazing coals flamed out:
    An intense fire consuming.
From his nose a billowing smoke came out:
    Bright flashes and fuming.

⁹⁻¹⁰ He split through the skies and then came down.
    He rode on a cherub and flew.
He sped on the wings of the wind all 'round.
    Black clouds 'neath his feet pushed through.
¹¹ His hiding place was dark and dim,
    dense clouds of rain in the sky.
They wrapped completely around him
    like a canopy to the eye.
¹² At the luminescence of his presence,
    dark clouds moved forward in sight,
with stones of hail and lightning large-scale,
    disrupting the shadow of night.

¹³ The Most High's voice boomed in the sky.
    With thunder the LORD caused jolts.
¹⁴ He scattered foes as he let arrows fly,
    routing with lightning bolts.
¹⁵ From the LORD's rebuke which rang mid-air,
    from the breath blast of his nose,
the valleys of oceans were laid bare,
    the foundations of earth were exposed.

¹⁶ From his high place he reached down and grabbed me.
    He pulled me from floodwaters' jaws.
¹⁷ He saved me from foes far stronger than I,
    right out of their hate-filled claws.
¹⁸ When they attacked me one daunting day,
    the LORD was my bolstering arm.
¹⁹ Since I was his joy, he lifted me out
    to a broad place free from harm.

²⁰ The LORD repaid my integrity.
    He spared me for I've done what's right.
²¹All the paths of the LORD have I trod.
    I've not disobeyed his light.

²²-²³ All that's required he's shown me.
    I'm faultless in life before him.
I've not cast away his demands.
    I've guarded myself from sin.
        ²⁴ The LORD repaid me for doing right.
        I've acted purely in his sight.

²⁵ You are faithful to the faithful,
    blameless to the blameless,
²⁶ pure to the pure, shrewd to schemers.
    ²⁷ To the proud you bring lowliness.
    To the humble you're a redeemer.

28 You, LORD God, give light to my lamp,
  you change my darkness to light.
29 With your strength in war, I can climb walls.
  or boldly advance in a fight.
30 You are perfect in every way, LORD God.
  your promises are tried and true.
You are a shield, a safe place to be,
  to those who take refuge in you.

31 FOR WHO O LORD IS GOD EXCEPT YOU?
AND WHO BUT YOU IS A ROCK SO TRUE?

32 You've strengthened me, perfected my way,
  prepared me for all my fights.
33 You've made me surefooted just like a deer.
  I can firmly stand on the heights.
34-35 You shield and save me, cause me to be great
  to fight against enemy bands.
My arms can handle a heavy bow.
  You've battle-trained my hands.
36 You make a broad place for my feet.
  They won't slip like shifting sands.23

37 I pursued my foes till they were destroyed.
  I smashed them and did not retreat.
38 I pulverized them. They rose no more.
  They fell down under my feet.
39 You've bolstered my power in battle.
  You made my foes kneel to me.
40 You made my rivals turn tail and run.
  I wiped them all out easily.

---

23 Lit. "ankles won't give way."

41 They cried for help, LORD, even to you,[24]
     but none were there to save.
42 I chopped them finely like dust in the wind.
     I stomped them to a mud-filled grave.
43-44 You've rescued me from warfare with people.
     You've crowned me king over nations.
Foreigners and strangers fear and serve me.
     They cringe and give adoration.
45 They lose their courage, come trembling to me
     from their fortifications.

46 THE LORD LIVES! TO MY MIGHTY ROCK BE PRAISE.
MAY MY SAVING GOD BE EXALTED ALWAYS.

47 You are the God who gives me vengeance.
     You put under me those who oppose.
48 You rescue me from cruel enemies.
     You lift me over my foes.
49-50 You've given great triumphs to me, your king,
     and shown me your love all my days.
So among all the nations, O LORD,
     I'll sing to you my praise.

     Your loyal love's there in each endeavor,
     to David and his seed forever.

Psalm 19

For the music director. A psalm written by David.

1 The marvelous, well-crafted heavens
     declare the glory of God.
2-4 Night after night,
     day after day,
without word or sound,
     their silence speaks,
          holds sway ...

---

[24] The Hebrew text says that the LORD did not answer them. This is understood and left implicit in the text.

reaching, preaching
to the whole world,
proclaiming him each day.

In the midst of heaven's canvas
there lies the sun ...
5 dashing bridegroom,
happy hero ...
its measured course to run.
6 Traversing sky,
none can hide from
its heat so fierce ...
once its journey's begun.

7-8 The LORD's **teaching is perfect**,
reviving the life.
His decrees are right,
giving joy not strife.
His laws are faithful,
making one wise.
GOD's commands shine bright,
giving light to the eyes.
9 The fear of the LORD is pure,
lasting forever.
His rulings are sure,
just and true altogether.

10 How much more precious than pure gold,
much sweeter than honey,
than honey oozing from a honeycomb
more valued than money.[25]
11 Your servant is warned by your word,
in obeying it, there's great reward.

12 Who can understand his sin?
Forgive me for those hidden within.

---

[25] This line is not in the Hebrew text but is logically implied.

¹³ Presumptuous sins, let me not make.
      May they not rule over me.
Then great rebellion I won't commit,
      and blameless I would be.
¹⁴ May the words I speak
      come from me with insight.
O LORD, my Redeemer,
      my Rock, my Might.
May my deepest thoughts
      be pleasing in your sight.

Psalm 20

For the music director. A psalm written by David.

¹ O king, I pray the LORD gives an answer,
      when a day of distress rushes in.
May the name of **Jacob's God**
      defend you and help you to win!
² I pray he sends help from his Temple,
      and from Zion comes all your support.
³ May he accept all your offerings as well
      as incense wafts through the court.   *Pause and reflect*
⁴ May he grant you all you've desired,
      and fulfill all the things you've planned.
⁵ May we raise up banners with joyful shouts
      for the victory won by your hand.
I pray all you want is granted
      as you lead us in this land.²⁶

⁶ The LORD is on high in his Temple,
      where he'll answer his chosen king.
By the strength of his mighty arm
      great victories he will bring.
⁷ Some by chariot strength will boast,
      some by horses' force are awed,
but we'll make our boast through trusting
      in the name of Yahweh our God.

---

[26] This line is implied but not in the Hebrew text.

8 We will arise and stand up strong,
     but our foes will collapse and fall.
9 Give victory, O Lord, to our king.
     Hear our plea when we call.

Psalm 21

For the music director. A psalm written by David.

1 The king celebrates your strength, O Lord,
     and your triumph in warfare.
2 You have given him all he desired
     and not refused his prayer.   *Pause and reflect*

3 You've graced the king with rich blessings,
     and placed on him a gold crown.
4 "Please guard me," he asked, ... You gave life:
     unending days with renown.
5 You gave him glory and majesty
     by winning each battle and fight.
6 You gave him perpetual blessings.
     Your presence brings him delight.
     7 He holds firm and trusts the Lord above
     because of the Most High's loyal love.

8-9 When battles start, you use great power
     to capture all your foes.
You consume them like a fiery furnace.
     You char them from head to toe.
By his wrath the Lord will devour them,
     destroy them with fire's flow.
10-11 Though your foes and their seed plot against you,
     you'll wipe them all from the earth.
Though they scheme wicked plans against you,
     their efforts will fail to give birth.
     12 When you target them with your bow,
     they'll quickly turn tail and go.

13 Lord, rise up in your might and devour.
We'll sing out praise to your power.

Psalm 22

For the music director. To the tune "Doe of the Dawn."
A psalm written by David.

1-2 Abandoned, desperate, restless,
     distanced from you ...
O God, don't you care?
     Don't you hear my words,
          when I groan by day,
          when I sob by night?
You've forsaken me,
     O God, my God.

3 Yet you ...
     enthroned Holy One,
          are Israel's praise.
4-5 Calling, trusting, saving ...
     Our fathers' fathers' story, ...
trusting, ... you heard them.
     No disappointment
          in you, my God.

6-7 Cast off, scorned, despised
     by all the people.
          I'm a worm, not a man.
They rail against me.
     Insulting, mocking, shaming:
          8 "See how he delights in Yahweh!
               How he trusts in him.
               Let him rescue him!"

9-10 Yet I, ...
     chosen, destined, intimate
          with you ...
               since womb, birth, breast,
               you've been my God.

¹¹ Trouble draws near.
>>No one to help.
>>Be near.
¹²⁻¹³ Lions, bulls – fierce bulls of Bashan!
>>Hordes and herds ...
>>>surrounding, threatening, encircling, ...
>>seeking to devour me.
¹⁴⁻¹⁵ Like water I'm poured out.
>>A broken pot's pieces am I.
>>>My tongue – parched, immobile.
>>>My mouth, my strength – dried up.
>>>My bones – disjointed.
>>>My heart – like hot wax ... melting.
>>To death's door you've brought me.

¹⁶ Surrounding, encircling, ...
>>these evil men,
>>these dogs, ...
>>>piercing my hands and feet.
¹⁷ Emaciated ... all my bones ...
>>on public display ...
The crowd, ...
>>staring, gawking,
>>>at me.
¹⁸ With a random dice toss
>>my clothes are claimed.

¹⁹⁻²¹ Be near me,
>>O LORD, my strength.
>>Deliver, rescue, save ...
>>>from the sword
>>>from dogs' claws
>>>from lions' mouths
>>>from bulls' horns.
Be near me,
>>O God, my God, ...
>>>YOU HAVE ANSWERED ME!

35

²² Before a crowd,
      your gathered throng,
I'll lift your name
      in praise and song.
²³ All of Israel,
      give him your praise.

All God-fearers,
      your voices raise.
Revere, laud him
      in all your ways.
²⁴ The LORD has heard
      and not despised
the suffering one –
      his pain, his cries.

²⁵ Before God-fearers
      my vows I'll pay.
Among the crowd
      I'll give you praise.
²⁶ The poor will eat
      and be content.
The GOD-seekers,
      their praise present.
Eternally
      their joy ardent.
²⁷ The ends of earth
      will hear the call ...
GOD to follow
      to give their all,
and each nation
      before Him fall.
²⁸ The LORD is he
      who reigns as king:
on each nation
      his power brings.

²⁹ All earth's great ones
      will bend their crowns,
all mere mortals
      will come bow down.
³⁰ A seed will serve
      the Lord always.
Generations
      in future days,
they will be told
      about his ways.
³¹ His righteousness
      they will proclaim
to future ones:
      unborn, no name.
A Lord who saves:
      Tell of his fame. ...
It is finished![27]

Psalm 23

A psalm written by David.

¹ The LORD's my shepherd,[28]
      my shepherd is he.[29]
For all of my needs
      he takes care of me.
² In fresh green pastures
      he makes me to lie.
Beside hushed waters
      he leads me right by.
³ My soul is restored,
      refreshed from on high.[30]

---

[27] Some scholars think that this connects to Jesus' statement on the cross: "It is finished" (John 19:30). It is a possible translation and has been translated that way, but other interpretations are possible like: "He has done it!" (NIV)

[28] Every line in the poem is five syllables. This is an attempt to translate the simplicity and succinctness of David's compact original poem.

[29] This repetition is added for rhythmic and poetic purposes.

[30] This detail is not part of the Hebrew text. It is certainly implied that his refreshment is coming from the LORD.

Along righteous paths[31]
>> he guides me along
to honor his name
>> to keep me from wrong.[32]

4 Though I walk through a
>> valley dark and drear,[33]
you're here beside me,
>> no evil I'll fear.
Your rod and your staff
>> bring comfort and cheer.
5 In front of my foes
>> you give me a feast,
anoint me with oil.
>> I'm filled and increased.

6 Surely your goodness
>> and unfailing love
>>> will follow me fast
>>> each day that goes past,
and I'll always live
>> in your house above.[34]

Psalm 24

A psalm written by David.

1 The LORD is he who owns the earth,
>> all things on it, each one who breathes.
2 On the waters he founded it,
>> and built it on seas.

---

[31] This could be a physical image like "straight paths" or the more spiritual "righteous paths". The Hebrew text is ambiguous and perhaps means both.
[32] This line is implied but not in the Hebrew text.
[33] The trad. rendering "valley of the shadow of death" is possible. But the image probably means "the deepest darkest valley."
[34] Lit. "house of the LORD," but "the LORD" is understood to be the referent of "your" because "the LORD" is the subject throughout the poem. "I" represents "David," "he" and "you" represents "the LORD" in the poem.

38

³ WHO CAN ASCEND THE LORD'S MOUNTAIN?
    WHO CAN STAND IN HIS HOLY PLACE?
⁴ Those with pure motives and good deeds,
    who've kept their promises,
        who from falseness turn their face.

⁵ Receiving blessing from the LORD,
    their Savior God will prove them right.
⁶ Such people are those who seek his face,
    who seek you, O Jacob's Might.³⁵   *Pause and reflect*

⁷ Lift up your head, you city gate!
    Be lifted up, you ancient door!
That the great and glorious king
    may enter strong and sure.
⁸ Who is this one who enters in?
    Who is this glorious king?
The LORD – powerful in battle,
    mightier than anything!
⁹ Lift up your head, you city gate!
    Be lifted up, you ancient door!
That the great and glorious king
    may enter strong and sure.
¹⁰ Who is this one who's walking in?
    Who is this glorious king?
The LORD who rules over all!³⁶
    Yes, he's a glorious king!   *Pause and reflect*

---

[35] "Might" is not part of the original text. However, Jacob's God is referenced as "the Mighty One of Jacob" in Genesis 49:24. So, the literal text "God of Jacob" implies he is the "Mighty God of Jacob," especially in the context of Ps 24.
[36] Lit. *Yahweh Tseba'ot* intertwines the ideas of royalty (kingship), power, and authority. It means "The LORD who rules over all" or "The LORD Almighty."

Psalm 25

א **(Aleph)**   [1] O LORD my God, I'm trusting in you.
ב **(Beth)**   [2] Let me not be put to shame.
Don't let my foes win and pierce me through.
I fully trust in your name.[38]

ג **(Gimel)**   [3] I know that whoever waits on you
will never be put to shame,
but shame will fall on all those who
make treachery their aim.

ד **(Daleth)**   [4] Reveal your paths, LORD, teach me your ways.
ה **(He)** and   [5] Lead me so your truth I can see.
ו **(Waw)**   I hope in you all of my days.
You're the God who sets me free.
ז **(Zayin)**   [6] Remember, LORD, your great love as always,
your mercy so rich towards me.
ח **(Heth)**   [7] My youthful sins, blot out from above,
my erring like a wandering star.[39]
Think about me, LORD, with your loyal love,
for you are good, it's who you are.

ט **(Teth)**   [8] The LORD is good and does what is right,
so he teaches sinners his ways.
י **(Yodh)**   [9] He leads the humble to be just in his sight.
He instructs them well all their days.
כ **(Kaph)**   [10] To those who keep his agreement and laws,
his ways brim with a love spread wide.
ל **(Lamedh)**   [11] LORD, for your name's honor and cause,
forgive all my sins multiplied.

---

[37] This is an acrostic psalm in Hebrew. It follows verse-by-verse the order of the Hebrew alphabet. The first verse starts with a word that begins with *aleph*, the second verse *beth*, etc. See the Introduction.

[38] Trusting in your name is not in the Hebrew text, but David trusts in the LORD (v 1) and speaks of the LORD's name in v 11. "Piercing me through" is also not in the Hebrew text but added for dramatic effect.

[39] "From above" is implied but not in the Hebrew text. The wandering star metaphor is used to describe the psalmist's rebellious ways.

מ (Mem)	12 Who are those who reverence the LORD? He will lead them by the hand.
נ (Nun)	13 They'll thrive as they live a life above board, and their offspring will own the land.
ס (Samekh)	14 To those who revere him the LORD speaks, to them he reveals his promise.
ע (Ayin)	15 It's the LORD himself whom I'll seek. Each trap set for me goes amiss.
פ (Pe)	16 Turn to me, God, have mercy on me, for I'm alone and oppressed.
צ (Tsadhe)	17 From all these anxieties set me free, save me from this distress.
ק (Qoph)	18 Forgive all my sins, this is my plea. Look at my strife and duress.
ר (Resh)	19 See how my many foes detest me, and how they seek to oppress.
שׂ/שׁ (Sin/Shin)	20 Watch over my life and deliver me. Let me not be put to shame. You are my refuge, to you I flee from those who seek to maim.40
ת (Taw)	21 May uprightness and virtue guard me because I hope in you. 22 O God, arise and set Israel free, from all the distress they go through.

Psalm 26

Written by David.

1 I've put my trust in you, O LORD.
    I've not tripped even slightly.
Establish justice for me, O LORD,
    for I have lived rightly.

---

40 "Seek to maim" is not directly stated in the Hebrew text here, but is implied in the psalm as a whole through the various threats of violence to the psalmist.

² Look at my thoughts and desires, O LORD,
    and test me graciously,
³ for I'm mindful of your loyal love,
    and live by your truth zealously.

⁴ I don't spend my time with a liar,
    or mix with a hypocrite.
⁵ I detest a crowd of sinners.
    With the wicked, I will not sit.
⁶ I'll wash my hands of all my guilt,
    as I come near your altar, LORD.
⁷ I'll thankfully tell of your wondrous works,
    and let my praises be heard.

⁸ I love your dwelling place, O LORD,
    and where your glory shines.
⁹ Don't destroy me along with sinners,
    or those with murd'rous designs,
¹⁰ who devise evil plans with evil hands,
    whose greasy palms show their crimes.

¹¹ But as for me, I live my life rightly.
    Save me, may your grace break through.
¹² I stand here safe from all harm, LORD.
    Before your own I'll praise you.

Psalm 27

Written by David.

¹ I'll fear no one!
    The LORD is my light and saves me.
I won't tremble!
    The LORD is my place of safety.

2 If evil foes attack
  seeking to devour,
and enemies advance
  in their own power,[41]
    they will trip and fall!
3 If war surrounds me
  with armies in view,
I'll have no doubts,
  I'll trust in you.
    I won't fear at all!

4 One thing I ask the LORD for,
and this I want more and more:
  to live with him[42] each day, ...
to gaze on his splendor,
to worship and adore
  in his holy place, ...
    to seek him and his way.

5 He'll protect me in his tent,
shelter me from cruel **foes'** bent
  on a day of dismay.
He'll lift me o'er the warring bloc
and set me high upon a rock,
  high above the fray.
6 He'll lift me to victory
o'er the foes around me.
    Sacrifices with joy I'll raise.
I'll offer them within his tent.
To the LORD is their ascent.
    I'll sing with shouts of praise.

---

[41] This is added for dramatic effect. From David's perspective their weapons are
of the world as he looks to God to win the battle.
[42] Lit. "to dwell in his house." This could be an image for experiencing the
continual presence of Yahweh because the temple was not designed to be dwelt in,
but to be worshipped in. The Holy of Holies represents the presence of God.

7-8 You've told me, O LORD, to seek your presence,
    so I seek you, my all in all.
Hear my voice, O God, and answer me.
    Be gracious when I call.
9 O God, you've been my helper.
    Don't forsake me, for I serve you.
Don't turn away in your anger,
    for you've saved me through and through.
        10 Even if my parents reject,
        it's me LORD you'll accept.

11-12 LORD, people oppress me.
Liars aggress me.
    My rivals will hurt me they say.
Give me not to their wrath.
Lead me on a safe path.
    Teach me to follow your way.

13 I know I'll live on and see
the goodness of GOD to me.
Be brave and strong as can be ...
    14 and wait on the LORD ... wait ...
    Yes, wait on the LORD.

Psalm 28

Written by David.

1 O LORD, my Rock, I call to you.
    Attend to my earnest cry.
If you are silent, I'll be like those
    who go down deep and die.
2 Hear what I say when I plea to you,
    as I pray and seek your face.
Listen as I lift up my hands
    toward your most holy place.

3 Don't condemn me with the wicked,
      with workers of evil and sin,
who speak friendly words with their neighbors,
      but hatch evil plots within.

4 Pay them back for the evil they've done!
      Repay to the utmost degree.
5 They care nothing about your mighty deeds.
      You'll crush them permanently.

6 Let praise rise to the LORD of mercy,
      for he's heard my earnest plea.
7 He is my shield and is my strength.
      I trust him and he helps me.
With all my heart I'll rejoice in him,
      and sing to him thankfully.

8 The LORD's people find their strength in you.
      You're their safe shelter, strong door.[43]
9 Rescue them, shepherd them, bless them, ...
      and carry them evermore.

Psalm 29

A psalm written by David.

1 Laud the LORD's glorious strength, angels on high.
      2 His holiness acclaim!
Bow down to his splendor and glorify.
      Praise his glorious name!

3-4 The voice of the LORD –
      over the waters,
            majestic, full of power.
The God of glory thunders
      over the mighty waters,
            a force to devour.

---

43 Lit. "refuge of salvation."

5-6 The voice of the LORD
     strikes Lebanon's cedars.
        He makes the cedars break.
He makes Lebanon leap like a calf.
     Herman hops like a young ox.
        He makes these mountains quake.
7 The voice of the LORD
     strikes with lightning flashes.
        He makes the earth to shake.

8-9 The voice of the LORD
     convulses the desert,
     twists the oaks,
        strips the forests bare.
It shakes the Desert of Kadesh. ...
     "Glory to God!" ...
        all in temple declare.

10 Over the waters the Eternal King,
     the LORD, sits on his throne.
11 Oh, that he'd strengthen all his people,
     and bless them with *shalom*.

Psalm 30

A psalm written by David. A song sung for the dedication of the temple.

1 I praise you, LORD, you raised me from a pit.
     My foes could not gloat over me.
2-3 I cried to you for help, my LORD God,
     you healed me and set me free.
You saved me from the dark throes of death,
     spared me from blackness to see.[44]

4 You faithful ones, honor the LORD's holy name,
     and sing to him praises in song.
5 For his anger lasts just an instant,
     but his favor remains lifelong.

---

[44] David literally describes being kept from *Sheol* and the Pit in this verse. These are references to the grave or the afterlife.

Weeping may linger through the night,
     but by morning, joy arrives strong.

6 When all seemed well, I said to myself:
     "I won't be shaken, afraid."
7 When I felt your favor, LORD, I stood strong,
     like a mountain unswayed,
but when you turned your presence from me,
     I was completely dismayed.

8 I prayed to you LORD for mercy,
     to you, only you I cried.
9 What gain would there be in my bloodshed?
     If I sank to the grave and died?
Will the dust proclaim your faithfulness?
     Will it give praise to you?
10 Hear my voice, LORD, have mercy on me.
     Save me from those who pursue.

11 From sobbing to dancing, lament to joy,
     you transformed all my dark days.
12 My heart will sing, LORD, and not be quiet.
     I'll give you eternal praise.

Psalm 31

For the music director. A psalm written by David.

1 Let me never be ashamed, LORD.
     I take shelter in you.
Save me because you're righteous in essence,
     and just in all you do.[45]
2 Hear now the sound of my cry!
     Deliver me soon, hear my plea.
Be a rock that protects where I lie,
     and a fortress safeguarding me.

---

[45] Lit. "in your righteousness deliver me." My translation reflects the two sides of righteousness: a characteristic of God (who he is) and his right actions (what he does).

3-4 You'll rescue me from the net they've set,
       and shelter me from this distress.
You'll direct my path to honor your name.
       You're my stronghold, my fortress.

5 My spirit I put in your hands.
       I entrust it solely to you.
You'll save me again, O my God.
       You're always faithful and true.

6 I hate those who embrace useless idols.
       In you LORD, I wholly rely.
7 In your great love I will fully rejoice.
       My anguish is seen by your eye.
8 You've saved me from each of my foes.
       You've set me safely on high.

9 Deep distress weighs me down.
       My eyes are melting from grief.
Agony within and without, LORD.
       Have mercy, grant me relief.
10 Groaning and sadness consume me.
       My years waste quickly away.
Flesh and muscles wither.
       Bones turn brittle and fray.
11 Neighbors despise me and mock,
       and my foes keep insulting me.
Best friends look away in disgust.
       Those who spot me in public flee!
12 Forgotten am I like a dead man.
       In shards am I from this strife.
13 "There's terror all about, all around him,"
       the crowd whispers, gossip is rife.
There are scores who scheme against me,
       wanting to snuff out my life.

14 But you are my LORD and my God.
　　In you I totally trust.
15 My fate now lies completely with you.
　　Save from my foes' deadly thrust.
16-17 Let me not be ashamed, O my LORD,
　　for I've called to you forcefully.
Show me, your servant, your favor.
　　By your love so loyal, save me.
Let wicked people be put to shame,
　　and be silenced endlessly.[46]
18 Let all their lies be silenced,
　　when they speak so pompously,
words against those who are righteous,
　　and used so contemptuously.

19 For those who revere and hide in you,
　　you've stored up good things which enthrall.
Many good things in full plenitude,
　　you give in full view of all.
20 You hide in safety those who are yours,
　　and keep them from schemes foes devise.
You place them safely under your wings,
　　to guard them from vicious lies.

21 Let the LORD be forever praised.
　　I was in a city attacked.
Then he saved me in astounding ways,
　　as his great love made its impact.
22 During a time of tense panic,
　　I thought I was out of your view.
But you heard my plea for mercy,
　　when I cried out for help to you.

---

[46] Lit. "in Sheol," that is, the grave.

²³ Love the LORD, all who are faithful to him.
    He protects those who stay true.
But he repays in full the haughty
    for all the evil they do.
²⁴ All you who wait for the LORD:
    be strong and heartened anew.

Psalm 32

A contemplative song written by David.

¹ How favored is the forgiven one,
    whose sins are pardoned, slate is clean,
² who's declared not guilty by the LORD,
    in whom no malice is seen.

³ When I did not speak about my sin,
    my bones rotted away,
as I groaned and moaned and suffered
    all throughout the day.
⁴ For night and day continually
    the weight of your chastisement stayed.
You sapped my strength like the sizzling sun
    beating on me without shade.   *Pause and reflect*
⁵ Then I made known my wrongs before you
    and I stopped hiding my sin.
I confessed and my guilt was forgiven,
    and now I'm free within.   *Pause and reflect*

⁶⁻⁷ You'll protect me in all my struggles.
    You are my hiding place.
On each side I'll hear all around me
    your songs of conquering grace.
So let all the godly pray to you,
    now while you can be found.
When floodwaters rise, you'll guard them.
    Surely they won't be drowned!   *Pause and reflect*

[8] You've told me, "I'll instruct you well,
and teach you the right way to go.
I promise to give you my counsel,
and guide your to-and-fro.
[9] So don't be without understanding
like an unyielding horse,[47]
who needs full restraints: bit and bridle,
so it does not stray off course."

[10] Countless are the pains of the wicked,
but the LORD's great love is true.
It encircles those who trust in him
in everything they do.
[11] You righteous ones, sing out to the LORD.
Rejoice in him, all of you.

Psalm 33

[1-3] You righteous, shout with joy to the LORD.
Give thanks on the harp to him.
Make a melody on a ten-stringed harp.
With a victory song,[48] break in.
It's right to play well and to sing well,
to praise him with vigor and vim.

[4-7] The word of the LORD is faithful.
By it the heavens were made.
By his breath, he created the stars.
Aptly his work was arrayed.
He gathers as one the rivers and seas.
The oceans in storerooms he's laid.
He loves what's just and all that is right.
His great love is worldwide displayed.

---

[47] Lit. "horse or mule." The two images are combined here for simplicity.
[48] Lit. "new song." Many commentators note that a new song is sung after a victory in battle. This especially fits the context towards the end of this psalm.

8-9 The LORD spoke and things came to pass.
 Let the whole world revere him.
He made a command, and it came to be.
 Let all the earth fear him.

10 The LORD quashes the peoples' schemes.
 He cancels the counsel of nations.
11 The LORD's counsel remains forever:
 good plans for all generations.
12 Favored are the ones whose God is the LORD.
 They're heirs as his chosen nation.

13-14 The LORD peers down from his house above
 on all the people of earth.
15 The Maker of all of their minds
 watches each deed, weighs its worth.
16-17 The war horse won't bring triumph.
 Its great strength won't hinder the grave.
The king and his army can't rescue,
 nor can the warrior save.
18-19 But the LORD honors those who fear him.
 He saves them from death and they'll thrive.
His eye's on those who hope in his love.
 In drought he keeps them alive.

20 We wait on the LORD who is our shield.
 He rescues from those who pursue.
21 In him our hearts fill fully[49] with joy.
 We trust in him through and through,
22 O LORD, may your love be upon us,
 as we place all our hope in you.

---

[49] "Fully" is added for rhythmic and alliterative purposes.

Psalm 34

Written by David. He sang this song after the time he pretended to be insane before King Abimelech, who ordered that he be sent away. So, David left.

א **(Aleph)** 1-2 I will praise the LORD constantly.
and ב **(Beth)** I will extol him with my voice.
I will magnify him unceasingly.
Let the oppressed hear and rejoice.

ג **(Gimel)** 3 Exalt the LORD together with me.
Let us praise him whom we revere.

ד **(Daleth)** 4 I prayed to the LORD and he answered me.
He freed me from each fear.

ה **(He)** 5 Those who look towards him shine with joy,
ו **(Waw)** and shame won't be their state.
ז **(Zayin)** 6 I, the oppressed one, called on God, was heard,
and was saved from a dismal fate.

ח **(Heth)** 7 The LORD's angel encamps 'round God-fearers,
and saves them from dire straits.

ט **(Teth)** 8 Taste and you'll see how good the LORD is.
Favored are those who trust him indeed.

י **(Yodh)** 9 You who belong to him, revere him.
He'll meet each lack for his seed.

כ **(Kaph)** 10 Young lions grow weak and get hungry,
but GOD-seekers have all that they need.

ל **(Lamedh)** 11 MY CHILDREN, LISTEN AND I WILL TEACH YOU
THE PROPER RESPECT THAT THE LORD IS DUE:

מ **(Mem)** 12 Whoever desires a long, fruitful life,
and seeks to live to their prime, ...

נ **(Nun)** 13 must never speak evil and lies,
and must keep their tongue in line.

ס **(Samekh)** 14 They must turn from evil and do good,
and pursue peace all the time.

53

ע **(Ayin)**	15 The LORD looks upon his righteous ones,
	and listens to each of their cries.
פ **(Pe)**	16 He's opposed to those who do evil.
	He'll bring about their demise.
צ **(Tsadhe)**	17 The LORD hears when the righteous pray to him.
	He rescues them from their distress.
ק **(Qoph)**	18 He is close to the brokenhearted,
	and saves the crushed and oppressed.

ר **(Resh)**   19 The righteous ones have many problems,
      but God rescues them from them all.
שׂ/שׁ **(Sin/Shin)** 20 The LORD protects their bones, none are broken.
      Yes, add them up, sum them all.
ת **(Taw)**   21 The wicked are killed by their own evil deeds.
      The just one's foes are judged in the end.
    22 The LORD will redeem his servants' lives.
      Those who trust him won't be condemned.

Psalm 35

Written by David.

1-2 O LORD, fight this fight, wage this battle
    for foes attack me, assail!
Put on your armor and grasp your shield.
    Come help for they thrash and flail!
3 Hold forth your war axe, thrust forth your spear,
    and save so I'll prevail!

    4 May they be ashamed and dishonored:
        those plotting to waylay me.
    May they be turned back and humbled:
        those seeking to slay me.
    5 May they be chased by GOD's angel,
        swept away like wind-blown chaff.
    6 May they be pursued by his angel,
        along a slick, somber path.
    7 I did them no wrong, but they dug pits,
        and entrapped where none set free.
    8 So, I bid you LORD: Trap and destroy them
        with the traps they've set for me.

And in the pit that they made for capture,
    may ruin be what they see.

9-10 I rejoice in you LORD who saves me.
No one's like you or ever can be.⁵⁰
    You deliver the poor from strong foes,
    the needy from thieves who oppose.
I affirm this with all that's in me.

11 Savage witnesses rise against me,
    accuse me of crimes I don't know.
12 They pay me back evil for good,
    forsake me to grief and woe.
13-14 But when they were sick, I was sad for them.
    I mourned as for my brother.
I truly prayed, even fasted for them,
    I grieved as for my mother.
15-16 Yet when I faltered, they laughed together.
    With mocking they slandered me.
The godless showed evil intentions,
    and attacked me constantly.

17 How long will you stand on the sidelines, Lord?
    Please save me from these lions!
18 I'll give thanks and praise to you
    before the crowds in Zion.
19-21 My foes are quick to accuse me of wrong.
    "Hah! We saw him do it!" they cry.
Let not those who ferociously hate me,
    mock me while winking the eye.
They plot against the peaceful ones
    who in the country lie.

---

⁵⁰ "or every can be" is implied but not stated in the Hebrew text.

²²⁻²³ Be close to me, fight on my behalf!
     Defend me, my Lord God!
O LORD don't be quiet! You see
     how they scheme, how they prod.
²⁴ Show that I'm right by your standards, LORD.
     Let them not boast over me.
²⁵ Let them not say to themselves "Hurray!
     We've devoured him easily."

²⁶ May those who lift themselves high over me
     with shame and reproach be clothed.
May those who rejoiced at my suffering
     be ashamed and brought low.
²⁷ May my friends who sought my favor
     cry out for joy and express.
May they ever praise the LORD who's great,
     who cheers for my success.

²⁸ I'll declare your justice as my theme song,
and proclaim your praise all the day long.

Psalm 36

For the music director. Written by David, the LORD's servant.

¹ God has inspired my thinking
     about wicked people and sin.
They have no respect, no fear of God.
     It's absent from deep within.
² They're too full of self and pride
     to see or hate their sin.
³ They refuse to do good and act wisely.
     With their mouths they tell evil lies.
⁴ They think up dark plans in the night.
     Sin's way they refuse to despise.
⁵ Your love extends to heaven, LORD.
     Your truth ascends to the skies.

⁶ Your justice is mighty like mountains.
   Your judgments are ocean size.
O LORD, all beasts and people you've made,
   they're cared for under your eyes.
⁷⁻⁸ In your house we are filled with provisions.
   We swallow streams of delight.
How precious, O LORD, is your loyal love!
   You protect us in your sight.
⁹ In you alone is the wellspring of life.
   We see by means of your light.

¹⁰ O LORD, keep showing your love to your own.
   To the just show ways that are right.
¹¹ Let not the prideful trample on me,
   nor the wicked put me to flight.
¹² See how the wicked are thrown down,
   unable to stand upright.

Psalm 37

Written by David.

א (Aleph)   ¹ Don't worry because of wrongdoers.
   Don't envy the evil throng.
² Like green plants they'll wilt away quickly.
   Like grass they'll fade before long.

ב (Beth)   ³ Trust the LORD, feed on truth, and do good,
   and live safely in the land.
⁴ Find your joy in the LORD himself.
   He'll give you your heart's demand.

ג (Gimel)   ⁵ Commit all you do to the LORD.
   Rely on him, and he'll help you.
⁶ Your innocence and acquittal like light
   will brightly shine into view.

ד (Daleth)   ⁷ Don't worry about evil schemers
   who seem to prosper, upstage.
Quietly trust in the LORD.
   ⁸ Don't be angry, turn from rage.
Worry leads to harm and discord.

ה **(He)** 9 Evil ones will be destroyed by God's hand.
But those who wait on the LORD
will be heirs in the land.

ו **(Waw)** 10 The wicked will be gone in due time.
If you search, they won't be found.
11 But the oppressed will be heirs in the land.
Peace they'll enjoy without bound.

ז **(Zayin)** 12 Evil ones scheme against just ones,
and seethe against them in hate.
13 But the Lord laughs knowing what comes:
In time they'll meet their fate.

ח **(Heth)** 14 Evil ones make ready their attack:
They unsheathe their swords, bend bows
against the oppressed and all those held back,
to kill the just ones with blows.
15 But their swords will pierce their own hearts,
and broken will be their bows.

ט **(Teth)** 16 It is better to be righteous yet poor
than rich yet vile in God's sight.
17 The strength of the wicked will be crushed,
but GOD helps those who do right.

י **(Yodh)** 18 The LORD takes care of those who are godly.
They're ever heirs of salvation.
19 They won't be ashamed, when times are bad.
He'll feed them in times of starvation.

כ **(Kaph)** 20 But those who are wicked will one day die.
They'll fade away like a flower.
The LORD's foes will vanish fast like smoke.
In the end they'll be devoured.

ל (Lamedh) ²¹ Evil ones borrow and do not pay back,
  but just ones give from the heart.
²² Those blessed by the LORD will possess the land,
  and those cursed: Death is their part.

מ (Mem) ²³ The LORD directs the steps of those
  who take pleasure in his way.
²⁴ Though they might trip, they will not fall,
  for he steadies them in life's fray.

נ (Nun) ²⁵ Whether in youth nor now in old age,
  I have never ever found
the righteous abandoned by the LORD,
  or their offspring begging 'round.
²⁶ They're always gracious, lending to others,
  their children's blessings abound.

ס (Samekh) ²⁷ Stop doing what's evil and do what's good,
  and you'll live in the land always.
²⁸ The Lord won't abandon his holy ones
  for he loves justice each day.
All wrongdoers will be wiped out fully.
  The wicked's seed passes away.
²⁹ Yet God's people will be heirs in the land,
  and in it they'll ever stay.

פ (Pe) ³⁰ From the tongue of the godly comes wise words,
  and they teach others right from wrong.
³¹ The instruction of God is in their hearts.
  They won't trip as they go along.

צ (Tsadhe) ³² The wicked ones target the godly ones,
  aiming to kill them, how vile!
³³ The LORD will protect the righteous ones.
  They won't be condemned at trial.

ק **(Qoph)** 34 Wait on the LORD and do what he says.
             He'll lift you up, give you the land.
          When the LORD wipes out the wicked,
             you'll see what he wrought by his hand.

ר **(Resh)** 35 I once saw a violent, wicked man
             grow strong like a tree in good ground.
          36 But soon upon query I'd heard he died.
             Yes, nowhere was he to be found.

שׂ/שׁ **(Sin/Shin)** 37 There's a future for those who love peace.
             Take note of those honest and good.
          38 There's no future for those who rebel.
             They're cut off as only God could.

ת **(Taw)** 39 Yet the LORD delivers his faithful ones.
             He's their strength through all of life's trials.
          40 He helps them and saves them from wicked ones.
             They're safe from the enemies' wiles.

Psalm 38

A psalm of remembrance. Written by David.

1 Don't chasten me, LORD, in your anger.
     Don't punish me in your rage.
2 Your power has pressed down upon me.
     Your arrows have pierced my rib cage.

3-8 I'm racked in pain, ...
     back bent, eyeing the ground,
unending strain, ...
     weakness and fatigue abound.
Searing pain in my bones,
     whole body aching, fire burning inside.
Festering stinking wounds,
     completely crushed as if I died.
My guilt overwhelms me,
     a burden too great to bear.

I groan with a heart full of anguish,
        deeply mourning as pains flair.
You rage because of my foolish sins.
        Profound is my despair.

9 O Lord, you know my deepest desires.
        My groans aren't secret from you.
10 My heart is racing, I'm falling apart.
        My vision has gone askew.
11 Because of my sickness, my friends and neighbors
        distance themselves from me.
12 My menacing foes try to kill me with traps.
        All day they plot cagily.
13 But I stay silent to all of their threats,
        like one unable to speak.
14 I choose to hear nothing of what they say,
        not answering their critique.

15 O LORD, I'm waiting for you.
        O Lord, my God, you'll answer.
16 Don't let them gloat over me when I slip,
        and rejoice at my disaster.
17 I'm near the point of collapse,
        as I face ongoing pain.
18 But to you I confess all my wrong deeds.
        I regret all my sin and stain.
19 For no just reason a great throng hates me.
        They're mighty and threatening foes.
20 The good I do is repaid by their bad.
        The good that I seek they oppose.

21 Don't forsake me, O LORD, my God.
        Don't be distant from me.
22 You're the one who saves me, O Lord.
        Answer quickly my plea.

Psalm 39

For the music director. A psalm written by David for Jeduthan.

1 I told myself that I'd be cautious:
    I would not sin in my speech.
I'd muzzle my mouth measuredly,
    when the wicked came within reach.
2 I kept total silence, but all in vain.
    My angst within me grew worse.
3 The more I thought, the more I burned, then ...
    I spoke when about to burst:
4 "My life runs swiftly, LORD, show how it ends.
    I'm a vapor and so finite.
5 How brief and transient are my days.
    My life's nothing in your sight."
            THOUGH MAN APPEARS SAFE AND AT REST,
            HE'S A MERE BREATH AT BEST.   *Pause and reflect*

6 Each man like a shadow disappears,
    rushing vainly to and fro.
Wealth-stacking and pack-ratting,
    not sure to whom it will go.

7 So now, what do I wait for, O LORD?
    You're my hope, that's plain to see.
8 Rescue me from my rebellious ways.
    Don't let these fools reproach me.
9 I rest silent before you, not saying a word
    because this correction's from you.
10 But please ease my suffering, stop striking me.
    I'm worn out, exhausted, I'm through.
            11 You devour men's treasure chests
            like the moth that infests. ...
    You punish for sins against you.
            MAN'S A MERE BREATH AT BEST.   *Pause and reflect*

¹² O LORD, hear my prayer as I cry out.
   Don't ignore me as tears outpour.
I live with you as a stranger,
   just like my kindred before.
¹³ Stop gazing so I can have joy again,
   before I am no more.

Psalm 40

For the music director. A psalm written by David.

¹ I waited on you with patience, LORD.
   You looked at me and heard my prayer.
² You lifted me up from the mud and muck,
   out of a pit of despair.
You set me safely on solid rock,
   a place secure, tried-and-true.
³ You gave me a new song of praise to sing,
   a song of praise to you.
Many will see this, and trust you, LORD God,
   and bring you the fear you're due.

⁴⁻⁵ Your wondrous plans for us, LORD, are many.
   No one is equal to you.
If I counted your great deeds toward us,
   I would never get through!
What joy for those who leave pride and idols,
   and put their trust in you.

⁶ You take no pleasure in sacrifices,
   or offerings piled and fired.
Gifts and payment for sin by themselves
   are not what you've required.
But my ears are turned toward you
   to do what you've desired.
⁷ I said, "In the scroll there's words about me.
   I'm here to fulfill my part.
⁸ My God, I delight to do your will.
   Your teaching's etched in my heart."

⁹⁻¹⁰ You know, LORD, how I've been bold about you
   in all of the words I bring.
I talk of how just and faithful you are:
   Your salvation and love I sing.
Before your people gathered as one,
   I've not held back a thing.

¹¹ May your justice and loyal love guard me.
   May your mercy not be curbed tight.
¹² Countless dangers are gathered around me.
   My sins pile up, blur my sight.
They outnumber the hairs on my head.
   My courage has turned to fright.
¹³ O LORD, please bring me deliverance.
   Help quickly in my plight!

¹⁴ Humiliate and put those to shame
   who are trying to kill me,
and those who want to destroy me,
   may they be vexed and flee.
¹⁵ Bring shock and disgrace to those who say:
   "He'll fall, just wait and see!"
¹⁶ O LORD, let all who search for you
   be glad and celebrate.
Let all who love your rescue, shout always:
   "The LORD is very great."

¹⁷ Yet I, I'm oppressed and helpless.
   May the LORD remember me.
O God, you're my helper and rescuer!
   Don't hold back, come set me free.

Psalm 41

For the music director. A psalm written by David.

¹ Favored are those who are kind to the poor.
   You save them, LORD, when things are rough.
²⁻³ You protect them and keep them alive.
   You bless them when times are tough.

When sick, you heal them and make them rise
       from their cloistered confines.
You won't hand them over to rivals,
       and their fearful designs.

4 I prayed, "Heal me LORD and show your favor,
       for I have sinned against you."
5 My foes seek my death and wickedly say:
       "When will his life be through?"
6 If one of them sees me, it's just a façade,
       looking for only bad news.
When he leaves my house, he goes everywhere,
       with gossip to diffuse.
7 All who hate me whisper about me,
       they think the worst, and lies spread:
8 "He has a malignant disease!
       He'll never get off that bed!"
9 Even my trusted friend who ate my food
       has betrayed me and misled.

10 LORD, restore me so I'll pay back my foes.
       Please show your favor to me.
11 In this I know that with me you're pleased:
       Over them you'll give victory.
12 You've sustained me because I'm blameless.
       You're ever present with me.

13 Praise to you, LORD, Israel's God,
It's you we will always laud.
       Amen, may it ever be.

Book 2 (Psalms 42-72)

Psalm 42

For the music director. A contemplative song written
by the descendants of Korah.

¹ My whole being longs for you, O God,
  like a deer longs for a creek.
² I thirst for you, the true God who lives, ...
  to be in your presence I seek.
³ It's been non-stop, day and night, ...
  my tears have become my food.
As my foes taunt me all day and say:
  "Where is this God you exude?"

⁴ As I wholly give self to you,
  I recall, O God, this one thing:
Leading worshippers to your temple
  at the feast while joy songs ring.

  ⁵ WHY ARE YOU SO DEPRESSED, O MY SOUL?
   WHY ALL THIS CHURNING WITHIN?
  I WILL HOPE IN YOU, MY GOD AND SAVIOR.
   I'LL PRAISE YOU ONCE AGAIN.

⁶ In my deep despair, I remember you
  from the land of the Jordan.
I think of you⁵¹, O God, from Mount Mizar
  and the peaks of Herman.
⁷ Deep ocean waters⁵² thrash and splash,
  towering waves of the sea.
Your waterfalls smash, your surges crash,
  again and again over me.

---

⁵¹ It could be that the psalmist is writing from the north while in exile. The psalmist clearly seems to be in a situation of oppression from antagonists as reflected in vv 3, 9, and 10. But we do not know the precise details of the psalmist's context when writing this psalm.
⁵² Lit. "the deep," an image of violent, fearful, and deep waters, best represented as the open sea or ocean, or both, as here.

8 The LORD's loyal love rules my day.
>His song stays with me at night.
To the God of my life I pray,
>who leads me through this fight.[53]

9-10 The jeers and sneers of my foes break my bones.
>"Where is your God?" they say.
They taunt and revile me ceaselessly,
>all throughout the day.
Why have you forgotten me, O God,
>you who are my rock?
Why must I mourn and stay in grief
>while my foes oppress and mock?

11 WHY ARE YOU SO DEPRESSED, O MY SOUL?
>WHY ALL THIS CHURNING WITHIN?
I WILL HOPE IN YOU, MY GOD AND SAVIOR.
>I'LL PRAISE YOU ONCE AGAIN.

Psalm 43

(continued)[54]

1 Take up my cause, God, against evil men.
>Show forth that I am right.
Save me from this deceitful den.
>Rescue me in my plight.
2 You are my God and my refuge.
>Why do you toss me aside?
Why must I continue in grief,
>oppressed by foes who deride?
3 Send forth your truth and shine forth your light.
>Let them be my steady guide.
Let them lead me to your holy hill,
>right to where you abide.

---

[53] This line is implied as the psalmist battles in the trials of life. I understand v 8 to be the center of Pss 42-43 (see the note at the beginning of Ps 43.)

[54] There is no superscription for this Psalm, but most scholars believe that Psalms 42 and 43 were one psalm at an early point in their history, especially because of the nearly identical refrain in 42:5, 42:11, and 43:5.

4 It's there to the altar of God I will go,
>   to him, my joy and delight.
I'll praise you, my God, with the harp,
>   singing with all of my might.

> 5 WHY ARE YOU SO DEPRESSED, O MY SOUL?
>>   WHY ALL THIS CHURNING WITHIN?
>   I WILL HOPE IN YOU, MY GOD AND SAVIOR.
>   I'LL PRAISE YOU ONCE AGAIN.

Psalm 44

> *For the music director. A contemplative song written*
> *by the descendants of Korah.*

1-2 O God, we've heard our fathers' stories
>   about distant days of old.
When you moved mightily in their midst
>   with marvels and wonders untold.
You uprooted the nations before them,
>   and crushed them powerfully.
You planted your people in this good land,
>   and gave them victory.
3 It was not by their own sword or power
>   that they gained the Promised Land,[55]
but through your presence of light and might,
>   you graced them to make their stand.

4 You ordain victory for Jacob.
>   You are my God and King!
5 Through your name we trample our enemies,
>   and knock them back with a swing.
6 I won't trust in bow or sword to save me,
>   7 but you've saved me from my foes.
You've rescued us from those who hate us.
>   You've shamed them with your blows.

---

[55] Lit. "land." "Promised" is implied.

8 We'll make our boast in God all our days.
　　We'll give thanks in his name always.　*Pause and reflect*

9 But now you've cast us off and humbled us,
　　and in battle we see defeat.
10 Those who hate us have stolen from us,
　　and from our foes we retreat.
11 You've scattered us to nations like seed,[56]
　　and let us be slain like sheep.
12 You've sold your people like cheap goods,[57]
　　and took no profit to reap.
13 To neighbors you've made us a laughingstock.
　　They insult us and jeer.
14 People disdain us and joke about us.
　　They shake their heads and sneer.
15-16 We hear each day our mockers' taunts,
　　avenging foes are they.
We're constantly disgraced and abased,
　　and shamed throughout the day.

17-18 All these things have happened to us,
　　yes, all to our dismay,
though your covenant we did not break,
　　nor did our thoughts go astray,
though we've always remembered you,
　　and not roamed from your way.
19 But you've devoured us in this place
　　where the jackals roam.
You've blanketed us with gnawing darkness
　　all around our home.
20 If we had prayed to other gods
　　or forgotten our God's name,

---

[56] "like seed" is implied through the verb "scatter."
[57] "like cheap goods" is implied in the context and provides a good parallel
structure to other elements of the verse.

69

²¹ you would surely have known it,
      for you know our thoughts, our frame.
²² But for your cause we're killed all day.
      We're sheep that are being slain.

²³ Wake up Lord! Why are you sleeping?
      Will you spurn us evermore?
²⁴ We suffer. Why are you hiding?
      We're oppressed, ... and you ignore?

²⁵ We crumple in the dirt face down.
      We collapse in grief to the ground.
²⁶ Rise, come to our aid, and rescue us,
      because of your love so profound.

Psalm 45

*For the music director. To be sung to the tune "Lilies." A contemplative
wedding song written by the descendants of Korah.*

¹ My thoughts overflow
with words apropos.
      My tongue is the pen
      that writes like wise men.
         My verses I'll sing
         as I speak to the king.
            ² You are the most handsome of men:
            Gracious words from your lips descend.
            Yes, God has blessed you without end.

³⁻⁴ Mighty warrior, with sword strapped on,
      clothed in royal splendor about ...
in your kingliness and majesty...
      to victory ride out ...
for the defense of truth and justice
      with humbleness portrayed.
Your amazing deeds are done
      by your power displayed.

5 Your sharp arrows will pierce
  your foes' hearts with white heat.[58]
Peoples will fall down before you,
  and lie at your feet.
6 O God, your throne is eternal.
  With a rod of justice, you reign.
7 All that is just and right you love,
  all wickedness you disdain.
Therefore, your God anointed you
  with joy and kingly oil,
pouring it more freely on you
  than peers who seek to be royal.

8 Infused are all your royal robes
  with cinnamon, aloes, and myrrh.
In palaces plush, the strings are plucked
  that cause joy in you to stir.
9 Daughters of kings are standing there.
  Your beautiful bride by your side ...
adorned with finest accents of gold,
  pure gold from Ophir supplied.

10 Bride of the king, listen to me.
  Let nation and home be ignored.
11 For your king delights in your beauty.
  Obey him. Yes, he's your lord.
12 The people of Tyre bring forth their gifts.
  The rich seek aid from your crown.[59]
13 The bride is aglow in her palace
  as she wears her golden gown.
14 In fine woven dress she's **brought** to the king
  with her bridesmaids escorting her.
15 As they enter the royal courtyard,
  they arouse with joyful stir.

---

[58] Arrows were often flamed for combat. White heat would indicate its intensity. "With white heat" is not in the Hebrew text.
[59] "From your crown" meaning "because you wear a crown" is implied.

¹⁶ Your sons will replace your fathers.
    The whole earth, they will rule over.
¹⁷ I'll make known your name to your seed.
    All will praise you evermore.

Psalm 46

For the music director. A special song[60] *written by the descendants of Korah.*

¹ When trouble comes ...
        to God we fix our gaze,
our refuge, our stronghold,
        our help always.

²⁻³ We will not fear
        though earth should shake
        though mountains quake
and sea foams near.

No fear say we
        though oceans roar
        and mountains soar
fall into sea.   *Pause and reflect*

        ⁷ THE LORD OF ALL IS WITH US.
        JACOB'S GOD IS OUR FORTRESS.[61]

⁴ God's own city:
        a river's glad grace
        in the Most High's place.
It is holy.

---

[60] Lit. "upon *alamoth*" which could be a style of music.
[61] The Hebrew text has this refrain in vv 7 and 11. This refrain is added here to provide a third refrain that makes the poem more balanced in English, more evenly dividing the verses before each refrain.

5 In her is felt
       God's touch, she will not shake.
              God will help her at dawn of day.
       6 Nations roar, kingdoms break.
He speaks, lands melt.

       7 THE LORD OF ALL IS WITH US.
       JACOB'S GOD IS OUR FORTRESS.   *Pause and reflect*

8 GOD'S works: look, learn.
       He destroys, causes fear.
              9 He stops wars,
       breaks bow, shatters spear.
The round shields burn.[62]

10 Cease striving, know
       that I am God.
              All the nations of earth
       will bring me laud.
Be still, bow low.

       11 THE LORD OF ALL IS WITH US.
       JACOB'S GOD IS OUR FORTRESS.   *Pause and reflect*

Psalm 47

For the music director. A psalm written by the descendants of Korah.

1 Every man, woman, girl and boy:
Clap hands to God, and shout for joy.
       2 The LORD Most High is to be feared.
       He's earth's great king to be revered.
3 He forces peoples under us,
tramples our foes with forcefulness.
       4 He chose for us the Promised Land.[63]
       For his prized Jacob it was planned. *Pause and reflect*

---

62 Or "chariots burn."

63 Lit. "our inheritance."

5 The LORD God ascends with great shouts,
     a victor's joy midst trumpets' blare.[64]
6 Sing praise, oh sing to God our King.
     Praise him who's beyond compare.[65]
       7 God as king reigns over the earth.
       With a thoughtful psalm, praise his worth.[66]

8 God rules over the nations
     from upon his sacred throne.
9 The nations' rulers have gathered
     with Abram's people, God's own.
For all earth's kings are his possession.
     Exalted is he alone.

Psalm 48

A song. A psalm written by the descendants of Korah.

1-2 How great is the LORD!
     How highly to be praised,
in Zion, God's city,
     a holy hill raised.
Beautiful is its height.
     All the peoples rejoice.
A great king's city,
     the place of God's choice.[67]
       3 God dwells in its high places,
       and guards its royal spaces.

---

[64] The ram's horn is mentioned here. It often has a nuance of victory in battle.

[65] "Beyond compare" is implied but not part of the Hebrew text.

[66] "Praise his worth" could be implied. It's added for poetic value, but is not part of the Hebrew text.

[67] This line could refer to "Zaphon" (see the NET Bible plus footnote) or refer to "the north" (see ESV and NKJV). NLT translates it as "the holy mountain" and CEV calls Mount Zion here "truly sacred." The understanding is that Mount Zion is set apart for God, "his choice."

4 A sight to see, as kings gathered and marched
      on the city together.
5 When they saw it, they were stunned,
      and ran away in terror.
6 Trembling came upon them, anguish, …
      like a woman giving birth,
            7 for you rose to demolish
            like the ships of Tarshish,
      using east winds on earth.
8 Just as we have heard,
now have we observed:
      the city of the LORD God of all,[68]
      the place of our God on whom we call.
God won't be deterred.
She'll always be preserved.   *Pause and reflect*

9 Here in your temple, O God,
      we think of your loyal love.
            10 Just as your name
            shows forth your fame,
      from so high above …
            your praise extends
            to the world's ends.
                  Your rule is with might,
                  and your deeds are right.
11 Mount Zion is rejoicing.
      Judah is walking on air.
Because you rule so justly,
      all your judgments are fair.
12 Encircle Zion and see.
      Her towers, enumerate them.
13 Her fortresses, walk through them.
      Her strong walls, appreciate them.
To her future seed, all that you see.
      All these things, communicate them.

---

[68] Or "LORD God Almighty" or "LORD God who rules over all."

¹⁴ This is our God we magnify.
He'll lead us always till we die.

Psalm 49

For the music director. A psalm written by the descendants of Korah.

¹⁻² All rich and poor, great and small, hear my words,
      whatever your history.
³⁻⁴ I listen well to proverbs. With my harp
      I'll explain a mystery.
Wise words will come forth from my mouth.
      My thoughts bring clarity.

⁵ I will not fear when trouble comes my way,
      when deception surrounds me.[69]
⁶ These wicked foes trust in their riches,
      and brag on their spending spree.
⁷ No one can redeem another one's life,
      or pay for it with a treasure store.
⁸⁻⁹ No ransom payment is ever enough
      to escape from death's door,
to escape decay in the grave,
      to live evermore.

¹⁰ Whether wise or foolish, all people die,
      leaving their treasure store.
¹¹ Though places they had named for themselves,
      the grave's their home evermore.[70]
¹² Yes, their human glory will disappear,
      like beasts they'll enter death's door.

¹³ For fools and those who rely on their words,
      this is the pathway they pave.   *Pause and reflect*
¹⁴ Their destiny's like sheep doomed to die.
      Death shepherds them to the grave.

---

[69] Lit. "when iniquity at my heels surrounds me." The image here is of sinful actions/people surrounding the psalmist wherever he goes.
[70] Following Septuagint, Syriac.

Their bodies will rot there far from their wealth.
    At dawn's light the just will prevail.
15 But God will rescue me from Grave's grasp.
    He'll be with me beyond the veil.[71] *Pause and reflect*

16 Don't be disturbed when people get rich,
    and their earthly goods are increased.
17 For their wealth will all be left behind,
    the moment they are deceased.
18 During this life they called themselves "blessed,"
    and were praised for their rich display.
19 But they soon will join their ancestors,
    far from the light of day.
20 Rich people who lack understanding
    are like beasts that decay.

Psalm 50

A psalm written by Asaph.

1 The mighty LORD God summons the earth, speaks
    with east to west in sight.
2 From Zion, the perfection of beauty,
    he shines forth so bright.

3 Our God approaches, and not quietly.
    He arrives with power.
A great storm roars around him,
    a fierce fire devours.
4 He calls the heavens above
    and the earth below
to witness against his people
    with a legal blow:
5 He says, "Bring my 'saints' who by sacrifice agreed
    to a love pact[72] with me."

---

[71] Lit. "He (God) will take me." "beyond the veil" is an interpretation of these words and refers to after this life, that is, "surely take me to himself" (NIV).
[72] "Love pact" refers to God's covenant (also v 16).

6 The heavens declare that God is righteous,
    and judges with equity.73   *Pause and reflect*

7 "My people Israel, I am your God.
    I have charges against you.
8 Your sacrifices and burnt offerings
    are always in my view.
    For this I don't charge you.
9 I don't need a bull from your farms,
    or goats from your flocks besides.
10-11 Each wandering bird in the wild is mine,
    and all living beings worldwide.
Each beast of the forest belongs to me,
    and cattle on countless hillsides.
12-13 I don't eat the meat of bulls,
    or drink the blood of goats, do I?
If I were hungry, I wouldn't tell you.
    The world's mine: earth to sky.
14 Make thank offerings and keep your promises
    to the God Most High.
15 When trouble comes, pray, and I'll save you.
    You'll honor me by and by."

16 But to wicked people God says this:
    "You don't have a right
    my decrees to recite
        or claim that you obey
        my love pact each day.
17 For you refuse my rod,74
    and my words you reject.
18-19 If you see a thief, you accept him
    in every respect.
You take part in adultery and tell lies,
and with your tongue you scandalize.

---

73 He is a "God of justice" or the text could mean simply "God is the Judge."
74 An image "rod" is chosen here to represent the "discipline of the Lord."

²⁰ You gossip against your brother,
and slander the son of your mother.
²¹ You have done all this, and I said nothing,
so you thought that I was like you.
But soon you'll see clearly my charges,
when my rebuke will strike you."

²² "So those of you who've forgotten me,
take heed to what I say,
or I'll come and destroy you fully,
and you won't be saved that day!
²³ But the sacrifice that honors me
is thank-filled adoration,
and the one who chooses to follow me,
I'll show my salvation."

Psalm 51
For the music director. A psalm written by David after Nathan the prophet went to talk to him concerning David's adultery with Bathsheba.

¹ Because of your great compassion, O God,
erase my sins totally.
Because of your covenant love,
grant your mercy to me.
² Purify me from my transgressions.
From my guilt, wash me clean.
³ For I recognize my rebellion,
and my sins are plainly seen.

⁴ Against you I've sinned, yes you only,
and done what's wrong in your sight.
So your judgment against me is just,
and you're proved to be right.
⁵ Since the day I was conceived, then born,
I've done wrong, been steeped in sin.
⁶ Yet you want truth, and teach me wisdom
in my deepest place within.

⁷ With hyssop wash me, I'll be cleansed from sin,
and I'll be whiter than snow.

8 Give me back days of mirth and gladness.
    Let joy from these bruised bones flow.
9 Don't even look on my guilt and sins.
    Wipe them out head to toe.

10 Create in me a clean heart, O God.
    Bring me back to loyalty.75
11 Don't drive me away from your presence,
    or take your pure Spirit from me.
        12 Bring back the joy of salvation anew,
        and give me the will to obey you.
            13 Then I can teach sinners your ways,
        so they'll turn to you their gaze.

14 Forgive me for shedding blood, O Savior.
    I'll sing of how just you are.
15 Help me speak, Lord, so I can declare
    your praise both near and far.
16 It's not offering and sacrifices
    that bring you delight,
        or I would give it.
        17 The sacrifices of God which are right
        are a humble spirit.
    A heart that is humble and contrite,
    you won't reject or slight.

18 Look on Zion with favor and help her
    to rebuild her walls tight.
19 Then with the gifts
    of the just you'll delight,
whether sacrifices or offerings,
    made in a spirit that's right.
Yes, bulls on your altar again
    will be offered in your sight.

---

75 Lit. "Renew a steadfast spirit within me."

Psalm 52

For the music director. A contemplative song by David. Written after Doeg the Edomite went to Saul and told him that David had gone to Ahimelek's house.

¹ O mighty man! Why do you brag of crimes?
  God is loyal all day long.
²⁻³ You enjoy evil more than good,
  lies more than virtue's song.
You plot to destroy, O great deceiver.
  Your tongue cuts like a sharp blade. *Pause and reflect*
⁴ You gladly attack with false words,
  O tongue that has betrayed.
⁵ Yes, God will destroy you eternally.
  He'll ruin you, strike you down.
He'll pluck you from this very world.
  On earth you won't be found. *Pause and reflect*
⁶ Good people will see this and revere God.
  They will laugh at you and say:
⁷ "See what happens to the man who
  does not make God his stay,
but trusts in riches and prospers ...
  His cruelty: his strong way!"

⁸ But I am like an olive tree in God's house,
  so flourishing and robust.
In the covenant love of God
  I'll always put my trust.
⁹ I'll give you thanks forever, O God,
  for all the things you've done.
And I'll proclaim⁷⁶ your good name,
  when your saints meet as one.

---

⁷⁶ Normally this word means "hope" or "wait," but some scholars think it means "praise" like in this context.

Psalm 53

For the music director. To be accompanied by flutes.[77] A contemplative song written by David.

[1] The morally bankrupt thinks:
    "God means nothing to me."
They are corrupt, their ways are vile.
    They act abominably.
        NO ONE DOES WHAT IS GOOD.

[2] From heaven God looks down
    on the whole human race
to see whether there are any wise,
    who sincerely seek his face.
    [3] All are corrupt and turn – each one.
        NO ONE DOES GOOD ...
    not even one.
[4] Do these evildoers not understand?
    They consume my people like bread.
They do not call on the name of God,
    but trust themselves instead. [78]
[5] God has terrified your enemies
    when no fear around them arose.
He'll scatter the bones of those raiding you.
    You'll shame them for God hates your foes.

[6] O that for Israel's sake out of Zion
    salvation would come!
When their God restores their lives,
    they will be glad for what he's done.

---

[77] "Flutes" or "round dance" or "according to the tune *mahalath*" are various possibilities here.

[78] This line is implied and not in the Hebrew text. Line 4c is lit. "call on God."

Psalm 54

For the music director. A contemplative song by David to be accompanied with stringed instruments – written after the Ziphites went and told Saul: "Isn't David hiding among us?"

¹ O God, by your name, by your might,
save me and show that I'm right.
² Hear now these words of my prayer.
Listen to my thoughts with care.
³ Aggressive cruel foes seek my life.
They're prideful and full of strife,
with no thought of you in their life.
⁴ But the Lord is he who enfolds me.
It is he who helps me, upholds me.
⁵ May evil fall back on my slanderous foes.
By your faithfulness slay those who oppose.
⁶ A free sacrifice, LORD, I'll give you.
I'll praise your name, so good and true.
⁷ From all trouble, you've rescued me.
I'll look on my foes with victory.

Psalm 55

For the music director. A contemplative song written by David. To be accompanied with stringed instruments.

¹ Hear me, God, as I lift my prayer to you.
Don't turn from my request.
² Be attentive and answer me.
I'm troubled and oppressed.

³ The wicked pressure and threaten me.
The shouts of my foes abound.
Besieging me with hateful anger,
they madly hunt me down.   *Pause and reflect*
⁴⁻⁵ So fear and trembling rise in me.
My poor heart pounds within.
The terrors of death are gripping my bones,
and horror claws my skin.
⁶ I said, "I wish I had wings like a dove!
I could fly away and find rest.

7 I could soar high to a distant place,
　　far off in the wilderness.　　　　*Pause and reflect*
8 I'd flee from this storm ever-raging,
　　and hide from its churning distress."

9-11 The city's full of strife and aggression.
　　My foes roam her walls day and night.
Deceit and oppression fill her streets,
　　while malice and trouble affright.
Destruction abounds, Lord, the wicked reign.
　　Confuse their plans[79] with your might.

12 If my foe was the one taunting me,
　　I could bear it, come what may.
If a rival had come and attacked me,
　　I could simply hide away.
13-14 **But it's you whom I trusted the most,**
　　with whom I'd often pray.
It's you ... my pal, my closest friend,
　　a man like me – no façade,
with whom I worshipped with others
　　in the house of God.
15 **Evil's at home** in the midst of my foes.
　　May their death swiftly arrive.
May they descend to the depths of **Death's throes**
　　into the pit alive.

16 But I cry to the LORD God my Savior.
　　17 He listens to what I express.
Morning and noon and night I lament.
　　He hears me in my distress.
18 He saves me in this fight, I'm not injured,
　　though throngs still rise against me.
19 The God who sits and rules as king says:
　　"I'm from antiquity.

---

[79] Or "words."

I will hear and I will humble these foes   *Pause and reflect*
  who won't change and won't fear me."[80]

20 My closest friend attacked his allies.
  He broke his word, betrayed me.
21 Like butter his creamy words poured out,
  like war his thoughts flowed free.
His smoother-than-oil words soon became
  like daggers piercing me.

22-23 You God, will send my foes to the pit,
  made for each killer and liar,
whose fate will be to live on until
  half of their lives expire.
Throw your load on the LORD, he'll support you.
  He won't let the just be dismayed.
My trust is completely in you, God.
  Never will I be swayed.

Psalm 56
For the music director. To the tune "Dove on Distant Oaks." A special psalm written by David concerning the time the Philistines captured him in Gath.

1-2 Have mercy on me, O God. I need you,
  for my foes pursue me ...
    with all their might,
    all day all night,
  relentlessly ...
  they press on to consume me.
    Many chase me, fueled by their pride,
  seeking to doom me.

---

[80] In the original text God does not speak directly (direct discourse). This does not change the meaning but gives a more vibrant message. This verse reflects one of two main interpretations for this verse.

³ BUT WHEN FEAR HAS ME IN ITS GRIP,
  I'LL RELY SOLELY ON YOU.
⁴ I TRUST GOD, PRAISE HIS WORD. NO FEAR!
  WHAT CAN THESE MERE MEN DO?

⁵ They distort my words and plot against me
  all day and all night long.
⁶ They spy and scheme, and hide in ambush,
  waiting to kill me, this throng.
⁷ In your wrath, God, strike down these hordes.
  Punish them for each wrong.

⁸ You've tracked my sorrows through the years.
They're in your book, none disappears.
They're in your bottle, all my tears.
  ⁹ When I pray to you, my foes flee.
  Through this I'll know that God's with me.

¹⁰⁻¹¹ AND WHEN FEAR HAS ME IN ITS GRIP,
  I'LL RELY SOLELY ON YOU.
I TRUST THE LORD GOD, PRAISE HIS WORD.
  WHAT CAN THESE MERE MEN DO?

¹² I'll give offerings of thanks to you, O God.
  I'll fulfill my vows to you.
¹³ For you've stopped me from stumbling,
  saved me from a graveside view,
so I can live in the light of life,
  walking closely with you.

Psalm 57
*For the music director. To the tune "Do Not Destroy." A special psalm
written by David concerning the time when he fled from Saul
and hid in a cave.*

¹ Have mercy on me, God, have mercy,
  for I take refuge in you.
I'll shelter under your wings for safety
  till danger's out of view.

² I pray to God Most High in this fight.
to the God who shows that I'm right.

³ He'll rebuke those who chase me, he'll save me
   by sending help from above.
God will send forth his great faithfulness,
   along with his loyal love.   *Pause and reflect*

⁴ There's ravenous beasts all around me.
Ferocious lions surround me.
   They're men with teeth like arrows and spears,
   with tongues like swords bringing fears.

      ⁵ MAY PRAISE BE RAISED, O GOD, FAR ABOVE THE SKY.
      THROUGHOUT THE WORLD MAY YOUR GLORY FLY.⁸¹

⁶ For my feet they've spread out a net,
and I am disheartened, upset.
   On my path they've carved out a pit,
   but they themselves plunged into it. *Pause and reflect*

⁷ All my thoughts, O God, are firmly fixed.
   With all I am I'll sing and praise.
⁸ Wake up, O drum! Rise quickly, O harp!⁸²
   I'll waken the dawn's first rays.
⁹ I'll thank you among the peoples, O Lord.
   Among the nations I'll praise you.
¹⁰ Your faithfulness is higher than the sky.
   Your love goes beyond our view.

      ¹¹ MAY PRAISE BE RAISED, O GOD, FAR ABOVE THE SKY.
      YES, THROUGHOUT THE WORLD MAY YOUR GLORY FLY.

---

⁸¹ Lit. "May your glory be above all the earth" or "upon the earth."
⁸² Lit. "the lyre and harp" here.

Psalm 58

For the music director. To the tune "Do Not Destroy."
A special psalm written by David.

¹ You rulers don't give fair verdicts.
    You don't judge people rightly.
² You rule the land with violence.
    Your thoughts clasp corruption tightly.

³ The wicked are born to sin, steeped within.
    They stray and tell lies year by year.
⁴ They're like venom that deadly snakes spit,
    like cobras refusing to hear.
⁵ Even though charmers of snakes play well,
    they refuse to open an ear.

⁶ My foes, LORD, are lions, fierce and robust.
    May their fangs and teeth be smashed.
⁷ Like ravaging floods, may they run off.
    May their arrows quickly fly past.
⁸ May they be dissolved into slime like snails,
    like stillborns who won't see the sun.
⁹ Faster than thorns made hot in a pot,
    he'll sweep them away, each one.

¹⁰ The just wade through the blood of their foes.
    When they're avenged, they're filled with mirth.
¹¹ All will say the just one's rewarded,
    and God justly judges the earth!

Psalm 59

For the music director. To the tune "Do Not Destroy." A special psalm
written by David concerning the time when Saul sent soldiers
to his house to spy on and kill him.

¹⁻² Defend me, my God, over uprisers,
    from bloodthirsty men who oppose.
Keep me safe from these criminals.
    Rescue me from my foes.

3 Cruel men, brute beasts, want to kill me, LORD.
      They've set an ambush for me.
I haven't wronged them in any way,
      no, not to any degree.
4 With no provoking they spring to attack.
      Awake, consider my plight!
5 Arise, LORD God, who reigns over all.
      Punish these nations who fight!
God of Israel, show them no pity,
      these renegades in your sight.   *Pause and reflect*

6 At evening, after prowling the city,
      like dogs they return with growling.
7 Hear their sharp words which gush from their lips.
      They think all ignore their yowling.
8 But you mock at these nations, O LORD,
      and laugh at their endless howling.

9-10 You, O God, are my refuge and strength.
      I'll rely on you and wait.
With loyalty you'll stand beside me.
      My foes' defeat will be great.
11 O LORD who shields us, don't wipe them out,
      so all will clearly remember.
With your power make them reel and stagger.
      Falling, may they surrender.
12 From their mouths have proceeded great sins.
      How they've cursed and how they've lied!
For all of these words from their mouths,
      may they be trapped by their pride.
13 Completely destroy them in wrath,
      so that nothing remains.
And all will know to earth's farthest reaches
      that God over Israel reigns.   *Pause and reflect*

14 At evening, after prowling the city,
    they return growling and yowling.
15 Like hungry dogs they scavenge for food,
    and if unsated, start howling.

16 Each morning I'll sing of your strength and love.
    Each trial you've pulled me through.
17 O God my refuge, how loyal your love.
    I sing these praises to you.

Psalm 60

For the music director. To be sung to the tune "The Lily of the Covenant." A special teaching psalm by David. It was written after he battled the Arameans of Northern Syria when Joab returned and killed 12,000 Edomites in the Salt Valley.

1 O God, you've renounced us in your rage.
    Restore us, whatever it takes.
2 You've broken us down and crushed us.
    You've split the land with quakes.
Repair the fissures, heal the wounds.
    Our land totters and shakes.

3 You've made us stagger as from wine's excess.
    We've had hardship like death's throes.
4 You've raised a banner for us who fear you
    to flee the raids of foes.   *Pause and reflect*

5 Answer my prayer to save your loved ones.
    Yes, rescue them by your power.
6 God has uttered from his holy place:
    "I'll triumph in this hour.
Shechem, Succoth, 7 Gilead, Manasseh,
    they all belong to me.
Ephraim will provide my warriors,[83]
    Judah, my royalty.[84]

---

[83] Lit. "the helmet of my head."
[84] Lit. "my scepter." A symbol of a ruling king.

⁸ Moab will I use to wash my feet,⁸⁵
　　and Edom belongs to me.⁸⁶
The Philistines I will soundly defeat,
　　and shout in victory."

⁹ Who'll take me to the armed and walled city?
　　Who'll direct my way to Edom?
¹⁰ Have you renounced us and our armies, o God,
　　not with us in war to freedom?⁸⁷
¹¹ Grant us help from those warring with us,
　　for mere human strength is vain.
¹² God will tread on our enemies.
　　With him a triumph we'll gain.

Psalm 61
For the music director. To be accompanied by stringed instruments.
Written by David.

¹⁻² O God, when I feel overwhelmed, listen.
　　I call to you. Please hear my cry.
Hear my prayer from afar. Lead me to you,
　　O Mighty rock higher than I.
³ For you've been my shelter and fortress,
　　where my foes can't come nearby.

⁴ Let me live with you forever, God,
　　and hide in the shade of your wings. *Pause and reflect*
⁵ A heritage for those who revere you
　　is such an amazing thing.⁸⁸
You have given me this heritage.
　　You've heard the vows I bring.

⁶ May the years of the king's life increase, God,
　　throughout generations, I pray.

---

⁸⁵ Lit. "a pot of my washing" or "wash basin" meaning it is completely subdued and held in contempt.
⁸⁶ Lit. "toss my sandal over" which is a symbol of ownership.
⁸⁷ Lit. "not going forth with our armies (into battle)."
⁸⁸ This line is implied in the poem's context but is not part of the Hebrew text.

7 May your true loyal love watch over him.
    May he reign before you always.
8 Then I'll praise you in song forever,
    as I keep my vows all my days.

Psalm 62

For the music director. For Jeduthun. A psalm written by David.

1-2 GOD ALONE IS THE ONE WHO RESCUES ME.
    I'LL NEVER BE SHAKEN OR STRESSED.
HE'S MY FORTRESS AND ROCK WHO SAVES.
    IN HIM ALONE WILL I REST.

3 How long will these rivals launch their offense,
    all of them trying to kill me?
They think: "He's like a rickety fence,
    like a wobbly wall is he!"
4 They plan to force me from my high post.
    They love telling lies about me.
They sing praises of me to my face,
    while cursing me inwardly.   *Pause and reflect*

5-6 GOD ALONE IS THE ONE WHO RESCUES ME.
    I'LL NEVER BE SHAKEN OR STRESSED.
HE'S MY FORTRESS AND ROCK WHO SAVES.
    IN HIM ALONE WILL I REST.

7 God is my strong rock where I find refuge.
    He alone honors and saves me.
8 Always trust him,[89] tell him your troubles.
    He is our safe place to flee.   *Pause and reflect*
9 All humans are full of lies and falsehoods.
    They're worthless I declare.
If weighed on a scale, they're less than nothing.
    They're just a puff of air.

---

[89] Lit. "(O) people". "People" is implied in the context as those whom David is addressing.

¹⁰ Don't vainly trust in oppression,
　　　　or place your hopes in stealing.
Though riches increase, don't trust in them,
　　　　though that would be appealing.

¹¹ These two things I've heard about you:
　　　　"You have power, O God above.
　　　　¹¹ O Lord, you have loyal love."
You repay each for what they do.

Psalm 63

A psalm written by David when he was in the Judean desert.
¹ O God, you are my God.
　　　　Sincerely I seek you
in this land that I've trod.
　　　　I thirst, I yearn for you
in this land dry and scorched,
　　　　where no water's in view.
² I've gazed on you in the holy place.
　　　　I've seen your glory and power.
³ Your love so loyal is better than life.
　　　　I praise you this very hour.⁹⁰
⁴ I'll give praise to you as long as I live.
　　　　I'll lift up my hands in prayer.
⁵ I'll sing joyful praise and be satisfied,
　　　　as with the choicest of fare.

⁶ On my bed throughout the night watches,
　　　　I reflect deeply on you.
⁷ I sing for joy in the shade of your wings.
　　　　You help me, you always come through.⁹¹
⁸ Your strong arm keeps me safe and secure.
　　　　It's you alone I cling to.

---

⁹⁰ "This very hour" is not part of the Hebrew text.
⁹¹ "You always come through" is implied elsewhere, but is not part of the Hebrew text here.

⁹ My foes who are seeking to slaughter me,
     to earth's depths they will descend.
¹⁰ To death they will go by the sword,
     a meal for jackals – their end.

¹¹ But with God's joy the king will be filled.
     All who swear by God will give praise,
while all liars' tongues will be stilled.

Psalm 64

For the music director. A psalm written by David.

¹ Hear my voice, God, as I lift my complaint.
     Protect me from threats of foes.
² Keep me safe from plots of the wicked,
     from schemes of those who oppose.
³⁻⁴ They attack without fear and quickly.
     They ambush with sharp tongues like swords.
At the blameless they aim their arrows,
     shooting them with cruel words.

⁵ They incite one another to evil.
     They plot secret traps declaring:
"Will anyone see what we're doing?
     ⁶ What a perfect plan, how daring!"
As they concoct their crimes, they smugly say,
     "Who knows our schemes so ensnaring?"

⁷ But God with his arrows will shoot them,
     so quickly with wounds severe!
⁸⁻⁹ By their own words, they'll be destroyed.
     All who see will shake with fear.
⁹ All will shudder and acclaim God's work,
     and marvel at his acts so clear.
¹⁰ The righteous will find joy in the LORD.
     In him they will be protected.
May all those who do what is right
     give him their praise undeflected.

Psalm 65

A song for the music director. A psalm written by David.

1 Even silence is praise to Zion's God.
    What we say in our vows we'll do.
2 You are the one who hears all our prayers.
    The whole world will come to you.
3 When overcome by my many sins,
    forgiveness you gave for them all.
4 Favored are those you choose to bring near
    to dwell near your temple walls.
We're pleased with your good and holy house,
    when there in your courts and halls.

5 Our Savior, through wondrous and righteous acts,
    you'll answer for us our plea.
You're the hope to earth's farthest corners,
    yes, even across the sea.
6 You set the mountains in place by your strength,
    and robed yourself with might.
7 You calmed roaring seas and pounding waves,
    and the nations who fight.
8 People from all the ends of the earth
    are awed by the wonders you do.
From the rise of dawn to the fall of dusk,
    jubilant songs break through.

9 You fill the earth with streams to sustain it.
    You make the land richly flow.
This water provides the people with grain
    for you have prepared it so.
10 You water profusely the waiting soil,
    and smooth each part of the field.
You soften the earth with your showers,
    and produce a bounteous yield.

¹¹ The harvest overflows from your goodness.
> Richness is what your path brings.
¹² You drench the pastures of desert lands.
> The hills wear joy bells that ring.⁹²
¹³ You clothe fields with sheep and valleys with grain.
> They burst forth and joyfully sing.

Psalm 66

A song for the music director. A psalm.

¹ Shout to God with joy, all the earth!
> ² Sing of his glorious name!
His name is of infinite worth.
> Honor his praise and his fame!
³ Say to God these words that are true:
> "Wondrous your works in our sight!
Your foes, how they cringe before you,
> because of your matchless might.
⁴ All those on the earth will worship you.
> All the world will praise your name.
To you they'll sing praises anew.
> All the earth knows of your fame."⁹³   *Pause and reflect*

⁵ Come, see God's works and what he planned!⁹⁴
> Wondrous his deeds for mankind.
⁶⁻⁷ He transformed the sea to dry land.
> They crossed with footsteps aligned.
He rules evermore with his hand.
> He is watching all nations.
Come let's rejoice in him and stand!
> No rebel agitations!   *Pause and reflect*

⁸ Come, praise our God, all who have breath,
> and sing his praises gladly!
⁹ He has preserved our lives from death.
> He won't let us slip badly.

---

⁹² Lit. "the hills put on the clothes of joy."
⁹³ This line is implied but not in the Hebrew text.
⁹⁴ "What he planned" is not part of the Hebrew text.

10 You've tested us, God, battered us.
    You've refined us as silver.
11 In your net, you have gathered us.
    We're burdened and bewildered.
12 Through fire and flood, you've tattered us.
    Yet you've blessed, you've delivered.

13 To your house I'll bring offerings.
    I'll keep each vow made to you,
14 vows uttered in my sufferings,
    honest promises and true,
15 fattened animals, slaughterings,
    these offered with smoke to you.   *Pause and reflect*

16 All who revere God, come and hear!
    I'll tell of his deeds for me.
17 To my God my cry was sincere.
    Praise filled my tongue loftily.
18 If sin I'd embraced in my heart,
    the Lord would not have heard me.
19 But God's heard my story, each part.
    He's listened attentively.
20 Thanks be to God who knows my heart,
    he's not turned aside my plea,
nor held back his love to impart!

Psalm 67

*For the music director. A song to be accompanied
with stringed instruments. A psalm.*

¹ O God, be gracious to us and bless us.
May your favor and light come fluoresce us, *Pause and reflect*
  ² so your way on earth may be known,
  your salvation to nations be shown.

  ³ O GOD, LET THE PEOPLES PRAISE YOU.
  LET ALL THE PEOPLES PRAISE YOU.
      ⁴ Let all groups shout out with glee.
      You judge peoples equitably.
      You guide nations sagaciously.
                          Pause and reflect
  ⁵ O GOD, LET THE PEOPLES PRAISE YOU.
  LET ALL THE PEOPLES PRAISE YOU.

  ⁶ The earth produces its harvest.
  Each of us our God has blessed.
⁷ May God bless us still year after year,
so all will fear him, far and near.

Psalm 68

A song for the music director. A psalm written by David.

¹ Rise up, O God, and cause your foes to flee.
    ² Like smoke drive them away.
Melt them like wax before a fire.
    May they die and decay.
³ But let the just be glad in your presence.
    Let them happily lift their voice.
Let them shout to God with fervor,
    as their hearts rejoice.

⁴ Sing to God who rides on the clouds.
    Sing praises to his name.
Rejoice in him whose name is Yahweh,
    the one whom we acclaim.

5 Father to orphans, a judge for widows,
   is God in his holy dwelling.
6 He finds a family for lonely ones.
   His care is so compelling.

He frees prisoners so that they prosper.
   What joys they are telling!
But in a sunbaked land will dwell ...
   those who are rebelling.

7 When you, O God, marched your people through desert,
   you led them on a pathway. *Pause and reflect*
8 The earth quaked. The sky dropped down rain.
   Your power was on display.
They made their trek with Israel's God who ...
   from Sinai revealed his way.

9 When your heirs grew tired and dry was their land,
   you sent rain, refreshed them indeed.
10 Your people lived there, and from your kindness,
   you fulfilled their every need.

11 The Lord speaks, and a vast throng of women
   bring this news of wonder.
12 Kings and their troops flee fast. And while home,
   women divide the plunder.
13 For those in camp who stayed to guard sheep,
   they'll share in the goods that were snatched:
the wings of a dove coated with silver
   with bright gold feathers to match.
         14 The Almighty scattered kings there
         like snow whipped through Mount Zalmon's air.

15 O Mount Bashan, you mighty mountain,
   covered with many peaks.
16 Why do you gaze at Zion, God's mountain?
   Like a monster your green eyes speak.

Don't you know that the LORD always lives there?
   He chose it: his mountain unique.

¹⁷ The Lord God came up from Mount Sinai
   into his holy place.
He came with billions of chariots
   into his sacred space.
¹⁸ LORD, you went up on high and took captives.
   You led in a line those ensnared.
And from your place of supremacy,
   you gathered gifts of warfare.
You received from all, even rebels,
   so that you GOD might live there.

¹⁹ We praise the Lord, the God who delivers,
   who carries our load each day.   *Pause and reflect*
²⁰ Our Lord Yahweh rescues from death.
   He shows us his saving ways.
²¹⁻²² The Lord God will smash the heads of our foes,
   who walk on a sinful track.
He says: "If your foes flee to deep seas,
   or Bashan, ... I will bring them back.
²³ Your feet can then wade in your rival's blood,
   while dogs' lips smack with a clack."

²⁴ O God, all can see your triumphal march
   to your holy place, my King.
²⁵ In front are singers, then musicians,
   and girls striking hand drums with zing.
²⁶ Praise the LORD God you gathered ones!
   Praise him who's Israel's source!
²⁷ Leading is Benjamin, the little tribe,
   then Judah's leaders, in force.
Then Zebulun and Naphtali's leaders,
   who follow in their course.

²⁸ Display your power and your strength, O God,
    as in past times you have done.
²⁹ In Jerusalem, at your temple,
    kings will bring gifts – each one.
³⁰ Scourge Egypt, the swamp beast. Scourge the nations,
    those bulls among the calves.
Make them submit with silver as gifts.
    For war-loving realms: Split their paths.

³¹ Ethiopia, … to God will raise hands.⁹⁵
    Bronze gifts will be brought from Egypt's land.

³² All you earthbound kingdoms, sing praise to God.
    To the Lord, let praises ring,   *Pause and reflect*
³³ to him who thunders as he rides,
    across ancient skies he swings.
³⁴ Acclaim God who reigns over Israel.
    He rules with power from the skies.
³⁵ O God you're fearsome in your holy place.
    You strengthen your people, your prize.⁹⁶
Yes, Israel's God empowers his own.
    May praise to him arise.

Psalm 69

For the music director. To be sung to the tune "Lilies." Written by David.

¹⁻² Save me, God! Deeper, ever deeper
    I sink down in the mire.
Murky waters rise up to my neck.
    My pending plight is dire.
In these deep waters, I can't stand up.
    A flood is drowning me.
³ My throat is dry, I'm exhausted.
    I cry to be set free.

---

⁹⁵ "Cush" is understood as Ethiopia. The image of hands raised (literal text) means in submission to God as quickly bringing tribute (gifts) or simply in worship to God.
⁹⁶ Israel as being precious to God (his prize) is implied elsewhere in Scripture but is not part of the Hebrew text here.

My eyes blur as I wait for my God ...
　　to meet my pressing plea.

4 Those who hate me for no cause are more
　　than all the hairs on my head.
My foes falsely say: "Pay for your theft!"
　　They attack and want me dead.
5 My guilt I can't hide from you, O God,
　　and you know my thick head.97

6 LORD and Master who reigns over all,
　　let those who trust in you
not feel ashamed because of my life,
　　and all that I've been through.
God of Israel, let your seekers,
　　not feel disgraced by me.
7 Shame and reproach I bear for your sake
　　to the highest degree.
8 I'm a stranger to my siblings,
　　to my children and spouse.98
9 I feel the taunts of those scorning you.
　　I'm zealous for your house.

10-11 When I wear sackcloth, and fast and weep,
　　crowds mock me and berate.
12 I'm the subject of the drunkards' songs,
　　scorned by those at the gate.
13 But I seek an acceptable time,
　　as I pray, O LORD above.
Help me, God, by your true salvation,
　　based on your loyal love.

---

97 "Thick head" ("blockhead," "bonehead," "fathead" – British) translates the
Hebrew word for "fool."
98 Although male terms are used grammatically, this can include the whole family,
here "my spouse."

¹⁴ Deliver me from these deep waters.
      Let me not sink in mire.
Save me from these foes who detest me.
      Lift me from straits so dire.
¹⁵ Don't let the fierce floods overwhelm,
      or depths overpower me.
Don't let these deep currents overcome,
      or the pit devour me.

¹⁶ Answer me, LORD, for your love is good.
      With mercy turn to me.
¹⁷⁻¹⁸ Deliver me from my enemies.
      Come close and rescue me.
Show your favor for I'm in trouble.
      Turn now. Yes, turn to me.

¹⁹⁻²¹ **You know how I've been** mocked by my foes.
      Their deeds, plain in your sight.
Their shaming and insults crush my heart.
      I'm helpless, nothing's right.
They offered sour wine to quench my thirst,
      poisoned my food to spite.
I looked for mercy, but none was found,
      for cheer, ... none was in sight.

²²⁻²⁴ May you pour on them your hot anger,
      and show them your fierce wrath.
Bend their back and blind them forever,
      so they can't see their path.
May their lavish spread become a trap,
      where they think all is well.⁹⁹
²⁵ Let devastation come to their camp,
      where tents have none to dwell.
²⁶ For they injure those you have punished,
      adding pain to **those you've hurt.**

---

⁹⁹ Based on the Septuagint for this line.

27 Don't let them be found as innocent,
     for crime waves they exert.
28 Don't list them with the just in life's book,
     for truths they controvert.
29 May your saving power shield me on high,
     for I'm stricken and hurt.

30 I'll give praise to God's name with a song,
     lifting my thanks on high.
31-33 The LORD does not spurn his captive ones.
     He hears the needy's cry.
More than an ox or bull sacrificed,
     my praise will please the LORD.
Oppressed ones will see this and rejoice,
     God seekers will be floored.[100]

34 Let earth and skies, land and seas, praise God,
     each thing from everywhere.
35-36 He will save Zion, build back Judah.
     His own will be its heirs.
They and their seed will live in the land.
     All who love God will dwell there.

Psalm 70

For the music director. A psalm of remembrance. Written by David.

1 Hurry LORD God, save me.
Help me now, come quickly!

2 May those who seek to murder me
     be turned back and ashamed.
May all who want to trouble me
     be disgraced and defamed.
3 May those be fully thwarted who say:
     "Get him now, we won't wait!"[101]
4 But for all who seek you and your way,
     may their joy resonate.

---

[100] To "be floored" is to be overwhelmed with amazement.
[101] Lit: "Aha, aha".

May your saved and loved ones always say:
"The LORD is truly **great!**"

5 God, I'm **poor and needy.**
Come quickly, make a way.
You're my help who saves me.
O LORD, don't lag I pray!

Psalm 71

1-2 To you, LORD, I've come for protection.
Because you are just, save me.
May I never be disgraced by foes.
Hear my plea, set me free.
3 Be my place of safety – rock solid,
where I can always flee.
You are my fortress and stronghold.
Speak now and rescue me.
4 Save from the might of the wicked, O God.
They're cruel as cruel can be.

5-6 I've trusted you from birth, Lord Yahweh,
from the womb when I was sprung.
You've been my hope and **confidence,**
from the time that I was young.
For your promise,[102] I praise you always.
7 You are my strength and protection.
I'm **a sign for many to raise.**
8 My life shines out as a witness to them.
I overflow with your praise.
And your splendor, I praise all my days.

9 **Don't reject or spurn me in my old age,**
when my strength sags like worn thread.[103]

---

[102] "**For your promise**" is implied because of David's "hope and confidence" in
God as mentioned in the earlier part of vv 5-6. It is added as an implied filler to "I
praise you always." It becomes a parallel line to 8c but is not strictly a refrain.
[103] The thread image is not in the original text but communicates the idea of
strength failing.

¹⁰ For my foes are plotting against me,
 and waiting to strike me dead.
¹¹ They say, "No rescue for him! God's left him!
 Let's chase him and attack!"
¹² Don't keep your distance from me, my God.
 Help me now! Watch my back!
¹³ Destroy and disgrace those accusing me.
 Spin them around in a daze.
¹⁴ Yet I'll never stop praising you.
 I'll keep on hoping always.
¹⁵ Though words fail, your rescue and right deeds
 I'll declare all my days.
¹⁶ Lord Yahweh, I'll praise your awesome works,
 and your right acts, yours alone.
¹⁷ God, you've taught me since I was a child.
 I'll tell of the marvels you've shown.
¹⁸ When I'm old and gray, don't leave me, God.
 I'll say to those after my time
that your power is remarkable,
 and your mightiness sublime.

¹⁹ Your just ways and deeds reach the sky dome.[104]
 O God, there's no one like you.
²⁰ You've made me endure times of anguish.
 Revive my life, take me through!

Though I plummet to the earth's deepest parts,
 you'll lift me up and restore.
²¹ You'll raise me up to a greater honor,
 and bring me comfort once more.

²² I'll exalt you God with harp and guitar
 for all your faithful ways.
O Holy One of Israel,
 I'll sing to you with praise.

---

[104] Lit. "the heavens," but the ancient Hebrew perspective is a dome in the sky.

23-24 You have saved me from my attackers,
  so I'm joyful, I applaud you.
You've acted justly and shamed them fully,
  so all day I'll laud you.

Psalm 72

Written by Solomon.

1 Give your righteousness and justice, O God,
  to the king, your royal son.
2 May he rule the people with righteousness,
  with justice, each grieved one.

3 Let peace and justice flow freely,
  from every mountain and hill.
4 Let the king help the poor and needy,
  and crush their oppressor's will.
5 May the people fear you forever,
  till the sun and moon pass.
6 May the king be like showers to earth,
  like rain drenching cut grass.
    7 After the days when he's crowned,[105]
    may the just thrive and gain ground.
    May peace and wholeness abound,
    till the moon cannot be found.

8 May he rule to the corners of earth.
  May he reign from sea to sea.
9 May desert dwellers bow low to him,
  and his foes be forced to flee.
10-11 May kings of Tarshish, Sheba and Seba,
  bring him tributes and gifts.
May all kings and nations bow and serve him,
  loyally without drift.[106]

---

[105] Lit. "in his day" meaning "during his days".
[106] This line is implied but not in the original text. God's desire is honest worship and faithful service.

¹² He will rescue those who cry out to him:
    the poor and those without might.
¹³ He feels pity for the weak and helpless,
    and saves them from their plight.
¹⁴ He'll rescue them from cruel oppression.
    Precious are they in his sight.[107]

¹⁵ May we his subjects say: "Long live the king!"
    May we pray for him always.
Take and give him the gold from Sheba,
    and praise him all our days.
¹⁶ May there be abundant grain in the land,
    from the hilltops, may it grow.
May fruit trees be like those in Lebanon.
    May the fields' grass richly flow.
¹⁷ May the king's name last forever
    like the sun in the sky.
May all nations prosper through him,
    and lift their praises high.

¹⁸ LORD God of Israel, we praise you.
    Only you do what amazes.
¹⁹ May earth ever be filled with your glory,
    and honor your name with praises.

Amen. Let praises flow.
Yes, may it be so.

²⁰ This is the end of the prayers of David, son of Jesse.

---

[107] Lit. "Precious is their blood in his eyes." A common interpretation is that "blood" refers to their lives.

Book 3 (Psalms 73-89)

Psalm 73

A psalm written by Asaph.

1 God is truly good to Israel,
    to those whose hearts are pure.
2 But I nearly slipped and stumbled,
    and fell from being secure.
3 For jealous was I of the prideful,
    when I saw the wicked gain.
4 Their life was a breeze with no struggles:
    a robust life, without pain.
5 They had no troubles common to man,
    not plagued by stress and strain.

6 So they dress with pride as a necklace,
    and aggression they wear as clothes.
7 Their eyes lust for endless profits,[108]
    and their scheming never slows.
8 They mock and make threats of violence,
    with pride worn around their girth.
9 They speak harshly against God on high.
    They bellow their thoughts on earth.
10 Even **God's** people drink up their words,
    as if their views had worth.

11 The wicked mock: "The Most High knows what?
    What we're doing, how could he know?"
12 These wicked! Take a look at their ease!
    No frets as their riches grow!
13 Was it for nothing I'd kept my thoughts pure,
    refusing to do what was wrong?

---

[108] This interpretation is followed by some translations (ex., NCV) and commentaries (ex., Ross, *A Commentary on the Psalms*). Some interpret it as "their eyes bulge with fatness," but this sounds like a metaphor for desiring riches. Others (see NIV) follow the Septuagint text as follows: "from their callous hearts comes iniquity."

¹⁴ While rebuke I've faced each morning,
        and suffered all the day long.
¹⁵ If I'd said things like these to others,
        your people I would have betrayed.
¹⁶ When I tried to grasp all these things,
        perplexed I became and dismayed, ...
            ¹⁷ till I came to your holy place,
                and their fate was clearly conveyed.

¹⁸ You've put them for sure on a slick path,
        and brought their downfall near.
¹⁹ How they're destroyed in a moment of time,
        and overwhelmed by fear!
²⁰ They're like a bad dream that fades at dawn,
        on waking, they disappear.

²¹ Oh, I've been so bitter, full of envy,
        churning within through and through.
²² I've been so foolish, so misinformed,
        a beast in front of you.
²³ Yet I'm ever with you, ever yours.
        You hold me and make me strong.
²⁴ Soon you'll lead me to an honored place,
        for you've guided me all along.

²⁵ Whom would I desire in heaven but you?
        Who but you on the earth?
²⁶ My body may fade, my heart may give out,
        but you're my heart-strength, my worth.
            With you I have an inheritance.
            With you, an endless residence.

²⁷ You crush those who are faithless to you, God,
        those far from you will die.
²⁸ But you Lord Yahweh are my refuge,
        and you are always close by.
For wonders you've done, I'll declare them.
        Of your deeds, I'll testify.

Psalm 74

A contemplative song written by Asaph.

¹ Rejection ...
>O God, spurned forever, it seems. ...
>>Why, oh why?

Vexation ...
>you heap on your sheep, such extremes. ...
>>"Why?" we cry.

² Think of the nation you chose long ago.
>Think of your heirs you salvaged,
>>and Mount Zion, your dwelling place.

³ March through these lasting ruins ... to and fro.
>See how the foe has ravaged
>>your holy house, your sacred space!

⁴⁻⁵ There your enemies chopped with axes,
>and screamed a victory cry.

They hacked your holy temple like trees,
>and let their banners fly.

⁶ They smashed wood carvings with hatchets and picks,
>and slashed the sacred to their shame.

⁷ They burned your holy house to the ground,
>and defiled the place of your name.

⁸ They scorched all your sites in the land, and said,
>"We'll sear them fsst with flame."[109]

⁹ We're left with no signs and no prophets.
>Will this always stay the same?

¹⁰ How long will our foes insult you, God,
>and keep despising your name?

---

[109] The created onomatopoetic word "fsst" is not in the Hebrew text. It means "completely" here. It also sounds like fast!

¹¹⁻¹² O God, you've been our¹¹⁰ King since ancient times.
    Why do you hold back your power?
On earth you've saved through acts and signs.¹¹¹
    Strike them I pray this hour!

¹³ You've crushed the heads of sea monsters,
    and split the seas¹¹² through your power.
¹⁴ You've squashed Leviathan's heads and left him
    for desert dogs to devour.¹¹³
¹⁵ You dried up rivers that always flow,
    and caused streams and springs to break through.
¹⁶ You hung sun and moon in their places.
    Night and day belong to you.
¹⁷ You set boundaries on the earth,
    and seasons you made brand new.

¹⁸ Don't forget LORD, how foes have scorned you,
    how fools have tarnished your name.
¹⁹ Don't turn us, your dove, over to beasts.
    Recall how we've suffered shame.
²⁰ Darkness and violence fill the land,
    so honor your covenant's claim.
²¹ Don't let the downtrodden be humbled.
    May the oppressed praise your name.
²² See how fools deride you forever.
    Arise God, fight for your cause!
²³ Don't forget your rivals' uproar
    which rises without pause.

---

¹¹⁰ Literally "my King." The psalmist speaks as Israel's representative.
¹¹¹ The Hebrew term here can be translated "acts of salvation." The idea of "signs" is implied.
¹¹² Although "sea" is singular in Hebrew, it can be translated as a plural or have the idea of ocean(s).
¹¹³ Hyenas **or** "desert dogs" is one of the interpretations of this difficult verse. See Tate, *WORD Biblical Commentary*.

Psalm 75

For the music director. A song to the tune "Do Not Destroy."
A psalm written by Asaph.

¹ O God, people proclaim your wondrous deeds.
    We thank you for your nearness.
² You have said, "At just the right time,
    I'll judge justly with clearness.
        ³ When the world and its people shake,
    I'll hold its pillars, none will break."
                Pause and reflect

⁴ I said to the wicked and arrogant:
    "Don't boast in your pride and might.
⁵ Don't raise your fists to me on high
    by bragging in my sight."
⁶ Exaltation should not come from the east,
    nor the west, south, not at all.
⁷ God alone judges and decides
    those who rise and fall.
⁸ Held in the LORD's hand is a cup of wine,
    full of foam mixed with spice.
He'll make the wicked drink it all down.
    How bitter is the price!

⁹ I'll ever sing praises to Jacob's God.
    I'll always tell what he's done.
¹⁰ God says he'll chop the wicked's strength,
    but strengthen the righteous one.

Psalm 76

For the music director. A song to be accompanied with stringed
instruments. A psalm written by Asaph.

¹ In Judah God is well-known,
    in Israel his name is great.
² In Jerusalem he shelters,
    in Zion he habitates.
³ He takes flamed arrows, shields, swords:
    all weapons ...
        and obliterates.   *Pause and reflect*

4 You are resplendent with light,
    more majestic than mountains,
ageless in our sight.[114]
        5 No warrior could withstand our sweep.
            Our fiercest foes have been plundered.
        They lie before us in death's sleep.
6 O God of Jacob,
at your divine snub,
        horse and chariot lay still – no peep, ...
        before us in a heap.

7 You indeed are fearsome.
        Who can oppose you
            when your rage is displayed?
8 You spoke your verdict from on high.
        The earth trembled, ...
            still and afraid.
9 You arose, O God, to judge evil ones,
        and save those on earth who are pained. *Pause and reflect*
10 Your rage against mankind brings you praise.
        Those who go through it are restrained.[115]
11 Fulfill all your vows to your LORD God.
        Let nearby lands bring their tribute
            to the Fearsome One.
12 He shatters the pride of the world's rulers.
        He terrifies earthly kings –
            each one, bar none.

---

[114] Following the Septuagint here: "eternal" or "ageless" mountains.
[115] One of many interpretations for this difficult verse. For example, "Certainly your angry judgment upon men will bring you praise; you reveal your anger in full measure" (NET Bible).

Psalm 77

For the music director. For Jeduthun. A psalm written by Asaph.

1-2 To you God, I lifted my voice, ... to you.
    Lord, you'll listen to me.
By day when trouble came, my heart sought you.
    I prayed fervently.
By night I lifted my hands without rest.
    No comfort came to me.[116]

3 I thought of you, God, and I was distraught.
    I reflected, then grew faint.   *Pause and reflect*
4 You propped open my eyes, I was so tired.
    I couldn't speak my complaint.
        5 I reflected on times long ago.
        6 I've searched my soul to and fro.
        I thought of my song in the night,
    and probed my mind high and low,
asking:
7 "Will the Lord reject us endlessly,
    or never again show his face?
8 Has his great love vanished completely?
    His promise gone without trace?
9 Has God forgotten compassion?
    Or in wrath held back his grace?"   *Pause and reflect*

10 Then I said, "What pains me most, O Most High,
    is to sense your power's on 'wait.'
11 I recall your wonders of long ago,
    the great deeds you actuate.
12 On all of your works I will ponder,
    on all of them contemplate."

13 O God, is any god as great as you?
    Holiness is your way.

---

[116] The original text could mean: "I continued steadfastly in prayer" or "I found no answer to my prayer."

¹⁴ You are the God who does wonders on earth.
      There your power holds sway.
¹⁵ You redeemed Jacob and Joseph's seed
      with a strong display.   *Pause and reflect*

¹⁶ The waters saw you, the depths trembled.
      They twisted in tortuous pain.
¹⁷ The skies rolled thunder. Lightning bolts blazed.
      Clouds spewed forth sheets of rain.
¹⁸ A whirlwind roared with thunder and lightning.
      The earth quivered and quaked.
¹⁹ Your way led through turbulent waters,
      yet no footprints did you make.

²⁰ You led your own like a flock to our land
by Moses and Aaron's guiding hand.

Psalm 78

A contemplative song written by Asaph.

¹ Listen, my people, to my instruction.
      Hear the words of my teaching.
² I'll tell you mysteries and enigmas,
      from ages past, far-reaching.
³ Things our ancestors passed down to us,
      as we've heard and learned facts.
⁴ Things we won't hide from our children
      of the LORD's awesome acts.
We'll speak of his deeds to those after us,
      his might and wondrous impacts.

⁵ For all the people of Israel,
      you gave teachings and decrees.
You instructed our ancestors
      to teach their children these,
⁶ so that in the coming generation,
      the children not yet born,
might know them well and pass them on
      to their children in turn.

7 Then they would trust God, obey his commands,
and not forget each great act.
8 And they wouldn't be like their fathers,
always faithless, always slack.
They were headstrong and defiant,
ever ready to turn back.

9 Ephraim's troops were well-skilled in war,
but rebelled on battle day.
10 They did not obey their pact[117] with God,
not heeding his law, his way.
11 They forgot the great deeds that he'd done:
his wonders on display.

12 He did wonders for their ancestors
in Zoan's plain, Egypt's land.
13 He split the sea and brought them through,
and piled up waters to stand.
14 He led them with a cloud by day,
and flaming fire by night.
15 He split open rocks in the desert,
and water gushed forth with might.
16 He caused streams to come forth from the rock,
and water flowed in their sight.
17 Yet they kept on sinning in the desert,
defying the God Most High,
18 willfully testing him in their thoughts,
craving food to satisfy.
19 The people dared God in the desert:
"Can God feed us here in this drought?
20 It's true that a rock was struck out here,
and streams of water flowed out.
But can he give bread and meat right now
in this barren place? ... We doubt."

---

[117] "Pact" and "covenant" represent the same Hebrew word in this psalm (see v 37).

²¹ After the LORD heard this, he raged at them,
    his fire broke out to devour,
²² for they refused to trust in him,
    and in his saving power.
²³⁻²⁴ But he gave orders to the clouds on high,
    and rained on them food to eat.
It was manna, the grain of heaven,
    scattered about their feet.
²⁵ Mere men ate the food of angels,
    profusely, "all you can eat."

²⁶ He stirred up an east wind with his might,
    and caused a south wind to blow.
²⁷ He sent them birds without number like sand,
    and rained meat on them below.
²⁸ All around them the birds downward flew
    in the midst of their campsite.
²⁹ He fulfilled all their lustful desires.
    They ate with great delight.
³⁰ But while the meat was still in their mouths,
    fulfilling their lustful desire,
³¹ God killed the youngest and strongest of them,
    for his anger raged like fire.

³² But on and on they sinned with no faith,
    despite the wonders he'd done.
³³ So he ended their lives in terror, ...
    fleeting lives under the sun.[118]
³⁴ When he killed some, they repented, sought him,
    wanting again to comply.
³⁵ They recalled that he was their rock,
    their Savior, the God Most High.

---

[118] "Fleeting" is the translation of the Hebrew word *hevel* "breath, vapor." It seems to indicate in the context that their lives were wasted, futile or temporary (quickly passing). "Under the sun" is more literally "their days", that is, their lived-out experience.

36 But they deceived him with all their words,
   and lied in all their ways.
37 For they were untrue to his covenant,
   faithless through all their days.
38 Yet through his mercy he forgave their sins,
   and did not destroy them all.
Over and over he held back his wrath,
   and refused to let it fall.
39 He recalled that they were passing breaths,
   just mortals, one and all.

40-41 How often they rebelled in the desert.
   They grieved God, causing him pain.
How often they tested the Holy One,[119]
   over and over again.
42 They forgot how God saved them from foes.
   They forgot his power and might.
43 In Egypt they forgot the signs he did,
   in Zoan, each wondrous sight.
44 He turned Egypt's rivers to blood,
   stained streams so they could not drink.
45 He sent flies to bite and frogs to destroy
   which brought them to the brink.
46 He sent grasshoppers and locusts in swarms
   to eat their crops like a disease.
47 He sent hail and frost to devastate
   their grapevines and fig trees.

48 He demolished their herds with lightning bolts,
   and their cattle with hail.
49 His flaming fury and rage burned down,
   his death envoys did not fail.
50 With full-vented anger he killed them
   with one last plague they were done.
51 He killed Egypt's firstfruits of manhood,
   each family's first-born son.

---

[119] Lit. "Holy One of Israel."

⁵² Yet he guided his people from Egypt,
     and led them through desert like sheep.
⁵³ He led them safely and banished fear,
     while their foes drowned in the deep.
⁵⁴ To this holy land, this land of mountains,
     he brought them by his strong hand.
⁵⁵ He pushed the nations out of their way,
     dividing the land they then "manned."
He settled Israel into their homes,
     and made them heirs of the land.

⁵⁶ They tested him, not keeping his laws,
     defying the God Most High.
⁵⁷ They were as faithless as a bent bow,
     like their parents in days gone by.
⁵⁸ They vexed him by worshipping idols,
     with sacred sites on high.

⁵⁹ When God heard their vain worship, he raged,
     completely rejecting his own.
⁶⁰ He moved out of his tent at Shiloh,
     and left them to dwell alone.
⁶¹ He allowed his strong ark to be seized,
     his splendor ... over to foes.
⁶² He let his people be killed by sword,
     inflamed with those he'd chose.
⁶³ Young hopeful grooms were destroyed by fire,
     songless virgins were forlorn.
⁶⁴ The priests? Pierced through by sword.
     Their widows? No time to mourn.

⁶⁵ Then like a warrior aroused by wine,
     the Lord awoke with new aim.
⁶⁶ He struck his foes, pushing them back,
     to give them lasting shame.

⁶⁷ God did not choose in Ephraim to dwell,
         nor Joseph's tribe did he think of.
⁶⁸ But Judah's tribe is the one he chose,
         and placed on Mount Zion his love.
⁶⁹ He built his temple like his home on high,
         fixed it like earth to last always.
⁷⁰ He chose David, from shepherding sheep
         to serve him all his days.
⁷¹ He took him from watching the flocks
         to tending his choice nation.
⁷² David shepherded them with pure motives,
         and wise navigation.

Psalm 79

A psalm written by Asaph.

¹⁻³ O God,
     your holy temple ...
         penetrated
         desecrated
             by unclean ungodly nations,
             disgracing your choice possession.
O Jerusalem,
     toppled to ruins of rubble.
         Bodies outspread,
         your servants dead, ...
     murdered by those who've brought trouble,
         by those they dread.
O Death,
     cadavers lie in blood
     outpoured like a flood.
         Food for vultures which abound,
         meals for beasts on the ground.
             Your own people devoured
             from those empowered.
         No gravediggers could be found.
⁴ Ridiculed by neighbors,
         despised by those around.

⁵ How long, LORD? Will your anger always rage? ...
       and your fury blaze like fire?
⁶ Pour wrath on those who don't know you!
       Pour on the nations your ire,
on those who don't call on your name.
       ⁷ They've consumed Jacob. It's dire!
And razed his home. Such shame!

⁸⁻⁹ Don't punish us for our ancestors' sins.
       Hear now, O God, our earnest prayer.
Help us, save us, for your name's honor.
       Have mercy, we're in despair.
Rescue us and forgive our sins
       for it's your name we laud.
¹⁰ Why should the nations demand us:
       "Where is this one – your God?"

Please avenge your servants' blood outpoured.
       May this vengeance worldwide be known.
¹¹ By your strength preserve those sentenced to die.
       Oh, hear the prisoners groan!

¹² LORD, repay these nations, yes seven times,
       for insults they've flung at you.
              ¹³ Then we your people, your pasture's sheep,
                     will give the praise you're due,
                     to each generation anew, ...
              moving ever forward in its sweep.

Psalm 80
For the music director. To be sung to the tune "The Lilies of the Covenant."
       A psalm written by Asaph.

¹ Listen to us, Shepherd of Israel,
       leader of Joseph's flock.
The one enthroned midst the cherubim.
       Shine on us en bloc.
² For the tribes of Ephraim,
Manasseh and Benjamin:

Rise up with your mighty power!
Save us from our foes and devour!

3 O GOD, RESTORE US.
    MAY THE GLOW OF YOUR GLORIOUS FACE
    DELIVER US BY YOUR GRACE.[120]

4 LORD God who rules over all, how long
    will your hot anger burn
against your people's ongoing prayers? ...
    against them at every turn.[121]

5 You've fed us with the food of sorrow,
    made us drink tears in full measure.
6 You've made us the scorn of our neighbors,
    and our foes mocked us with pleasure.

7 O GOD WHO RULES OVER ALL, RESTORE US.
    MAY THE GLOW OF YOUR GLORIOUS FACE
    DELIVER US BY YOUR GRACE.

8 You brought a grapevine out of Egypt,
    forced out nations there,
    and planted us with care.
9 You cleared ground in this new land.
    We formed deep roots here,
    and filled this new frontier.
10 The shade of our vine covered the mountains,
    our branches: large cedar trees.
11 We sent out our shoots to the River,
    and branches which reached the Sea.[122]

---

[120] The idiom "face shine on us" probably means "show us your favor." The meaning implies God's favor through his grace. The same idiom is used in vv 7 and 19 of this psalm.
[121] This line is not in the Hebrew text. It is implied in the verses that follow.
[122] "Sea" means the Mediterranean Sea and "River" refers to the Euphrates River.

¹² Why have you torn down our vineyard walls?
    Each passerby steals our grapes!
¹³ Wild boars and other beasts devour our vine
    as we watch with mouths agape.
¹⁴⁻¹⁵ Return to us, God who rules over all!
    Peer down from on high and see.
Take care of this vine you have planted,
    this son you've raised tenderly.

¹⁶ Our enemies have cut down your vine,
    consuming it by fire.
But this was a rebuke for your own,
    the object of your ire.
¹⁷ But give blessing to the man at your side,[123]
    the one you've strengthened, your own.[124]
¹⁸ We'll then not again turn back from you.
    Renew us, we'll trust you alone.

¹⁹ RESTORE US, LORD GOD WHO RULES OVER ALL.
    MAY THE GLOW OF YOUR GLORIOUS FACE
    DELIVER US BY YOUR GRACE.

Psalm 81

For the music director. A song accompanied by the harp used at Gath.
Written by Asaph.

¹ Sing aloud, shout for joy to Jacob's God,
    God the Defender you are.
² Start the music, strike the hand drums,
    strum the harp[125] and guitar.

---

[123] This Hebrew expression "man of your right side" is ambiguous and probably refers to the king, but some take it to refer to the nation Israel.

[124] Lit. "the son of man you've strengthened for yourself." This could be a veiled reference to the Messiah, but the verse is probably talking about the current Davidic king who is strengthened by the Lord.

[125] Modern harps are usually plucked and are large instruments, but ancient harps were probably more like two-feet long guitars, perhaps strummed and plucked.

3 Blow the ram's horn at new moon and full moon,
      announcing the festival.
4 This ruling from Jacob's God is just,
      and required for Israel.
        5 In Joseph's time he made it a command,
        when God led them out of Egypt's land.
        He heard words he did not understand.[126]

6-7 "God[127] said:
'I relieved the burdens from you.
      I freed you from brick laboring.
In angst you called, I brought you through.
      I tested you at Meribah's Spring.
From a dark cloud I answered you.   *Pause and reflect*

8 My people Israel, I rebuke you!
      If only you'd listen to me!
9 You must never worship another god,
      or bow to a strange deity.
10 I am the LORD God who delivered you.
      From Egypt I lifted you up.
Open wide your mouth, and I'll nourish you.
      Yes, I will fill your cup.[128]

11 But my people refused to heed my words.
      They refused to follow me.
12 So I let them follow their own stubborn ways,
      to seek their own fantasy.
13 Oh that my people would walk in my ways –
      that they would obey me.

---

[126] This is based on the Septuagint, Syriac, NIV84, and ERV. The idea is that Joseph doesn't understand Egyptian when he first arrives in Egypt. The "he" refers to Joseph both individually and to the nation Israel (Joseph represents the people). Most versions say something like: "I heard an unknown voice say" (NIV11). That interpretation introduces the words that follow as God's revelation.
[127] From the Septuagint, Syriac. See note at the end of v 5. Vv 6-7 clearly talk about Israel's Egyptian slave experiences.
[128] This line in not in the original text, but the image is consistent with the idea of God feeding his people.

¹⁴ If they did, I'd quickly defeat their foes.
I'd strike down all who oppose.
¹⁵ All who hate me will cower before me.
They'll always be filled with woes.
¹⁶ But I would feed you with the best wheat,
and from the best honey you'd eat.' "¹²⁹

Psalm 82

A psalm written by Asaph.

¹ In heaven's court God stands among "gods."
He gives a judgment and states:
² "How long will you favor the wicked,
and defend them with dictates?"   *Pause and reflect*

³ "Judge fairly the poor and orphans,
defend all those in need.
⁴ Rescue the weak and the helpless
from the wicked's stampede.
⁵ No one among you understands a thing.
You roam around in the dark,
while all the foundations of earth
shake and crumble apart."

⁶ This I have stated, "You are 'gods.'
You're children of the Most High."
⁷ But like all potentates you'll fall,
like all humans you'll die.
⁸ Arise God, judge this world from your view,
for all the nations belong to you.

Psalm 83

A song. A psalm written by Asaph.

¹ Don't be quiet, God, don't be distant.
Don't be deaf toward me.
² See how your foes are puffed up and proud.
They jeer and roar noisily.

---

¹²⁹ Lit. "with honey from a rock I will satisfy you."

3 They plot craftily against your own,
    the ones you love, your devout.
4 They say: "Let's slaughter this nation,
    so their name will be wiped out."

5 They've conspired together with a plan.
    Against you they've made a pact.
6 The Edomites and Ishmaelites,
    Moabites and Hagrites attacked.
7 Those from Gebal, Ammon, Amalek, Tyre,
    with Philistines in on the plot.
8 Assyria too had joined in with them,
    allied with the sons of Lot.   *Pause and reflect*

9 Like you did with Midian, punish them.
    Defeated were they and knocked down.
Like Sisera and Jabin at Kishon's Creek,
    your many victories abound.
10 You thrashed them soundly at Endor,
    thrown like dirt to the ground.[130]
11 You wiped out leaders like Oreb and Zeeb,
    Zalmunna and Zebah's right hand.
12 These Midian generals and kings who said:
    "Let's seize for ourselves God's land."

13 Like whirling dust, or wind-blown chaff, God,
    spin them around without aim.
14 As a forest is burned down by fire,
    or hills set ablaze by flame.
15-16 With gale-force winds, LORD, chase after them,
    and bring upon them great shame.
With a fierce storm petrify them,
    so they'll seek to know your name.
17 May they be forever terrified.
    May they die in horrendous shame.

---

[130] Or, "they became like dung on the ground" or "their bodies rotted on the ground."

¹⁸ May they know that only you rule this world,
the Most High ... Yahweh your name.

Psalm 84

For the music director. A psalm accompanied by the harp used at Gath.
Written by the descendants of Korah.

¹ LORD Almighty,¹³¹ how I love your temple!
² I long, yes yearn, for your courts to view.
My whole self shouts to the true God who lives,
as I sing with joy to you.
³ Even the sparrow and swallow build nests,
near your altars, ... their wings to rest.
They keep their young there to be near you,
my LORD God Almighty and King.
⁴ Favored are those who live in your house.
Your praise they always bring.   *Pause and reflect*

⁵ Favored are those who are pilgrims at heart,¹³²
those who find strength in you.
⁶ When they cross **through the Valley of "Weeping,"**¹³³
you provide them springs that renew.
The early rains cover the valley
with pools within it to view.
⁷ They will appear before you in Zion,
strengthened through life by you.

⁸⁻⁹ LORD God Almighty, please answer my prayer.
God of Jacob, favor our king.   *Pause and reflect*
Watch over our "shield," your anointed one,
who protects us in everything.

---

¹³¹ In Hebrew *Yahweh Tseba'ot* which intertwines the ideas of royalty (kingship),
power, and authority. It means "The LORD who rules over all" (see Ps 24:10) or
"The LORD Almighty" (also in vv 3, 8, and 12 of this psalm).
¹³² This refers to one or more of the three annual pilgrimages to Zion as prescribed
in the Law (Deut 16:16-17).
¹³³ Valley of "Baka" ("weeping") in Hebrew. It could possibly refer to the poplar
tree.

¹⁰ One day in your courts, O God, is better
     than a thousand elsewhere.
I'd rather guard the gate of your house
     than live in the wicked's lair.
¹¹ For the LORD God grants us favor and glory.
     He is our shield and sun.
He does not hold back any good thing
     for those faultless in what they've done.
¹² Favored is each who trusts in you fully,
     yes, you LORD, the Almighty One.

Psalm 85

For the music director. A psalm written by the descendants of Korah.

¹ You turned the tide for Jacob,¹³⁴ O LORD,
     you've wonderfully blessed your land.
² You took away your people's sins,
     and forgave with a gracious hand.   *Pause and reflect*
³ You turned back from your burning anger,
     withdrew your wrath that was planned.

⁴ Now turn to us anew, stop your rage,
     O God of our salvation.
⁵ Will your anger be on us always,
     throughout each generation?
⁶ Won't you come and revive your people,
     that we can rejoice in you?
⁷ Manifest your loyal love, O LORD.
     Save us through and through.

⁸ I'll hear what the LORD God says to his own,
     he promises a peace steadfast.
But may his faithful not turn back,
     to their foolishness of the past.
⁹ Surely, he'll save soon those who fear him,
     his glory with us at last.

---

¹³⁴ Lit. "turned a turning" could be a reference to bringing back from captivity or could be a more general idiom like "turn the tide" or "restore the fortunes of" (see Job 42:10). Even the more general idea could refer to a return from captivity.

¹⁰ Loyal love meets faithfulness.
Righteousness and peace kiss.
    ¹¹ Faithfulness sprouts up from the ground.
    From the sky righteousness looks down.
¹² Good things the LORD will provide.
Our land will have yields multiplied.
    ¹³ Righteousness will advance before the LORD,
    to prepare his steps on a path forward.

Psalm 86

A prayer written by David.

¹⁻² Hear my prayer, my LORD God, preserve my life.
    Though loyal, I'm oppressed, and in need.
I serve you and put my trust in you.
    Deliver me I plead.
³ O Lord, show me mercy and kindness.
    I call out all day to you.
⁴ Make glad, Lord, your trusting servant.
    My life is yours through and through.
⁵ You're good, full of love, and forgiving, Lord,
    for those who pray to you.
⁶ Listen LORD, to my prayer for help.
    I wait for you to break through.
⁷ When trouble comes, I know you'll answer,
    that's why I call upon you.

⁸ No other gods can compare to you, Lord.
    Your wondrous works I applaud.
⁹ Each nation you've made will bow to you.
    They'll glorify you and be awed.
¹⁰ For you are great and your deeds are stunning.
    In truth, only you are God.

¹¹ Teach me your way, LORD, I'll walk in your truth.
　　　Give me one goal:¹³⁵ to fear your name.
¹² With all my heart I'll thank you, Lord God,
　　　"To honor you always," ... my aim.
¹³ Your loyal love to me is so great,
　　　you've saved me from Death's¹³⁶ dread claim.

¹⁴ Violent and proud people, O God,
　　　have risen up to slay me.
They know nothing at all about you,
　　　and act aggressively.
¹⁵ But you, O Lord, show mercy and love,
　　　and you are slow to get angry.
Your loyal love and faithfulness
　　　are manifest so amply!

¹⁶ Turn to me and show me mercy.
Give me your strength and come save me,
　　　for like my mother¹³⁷ I serve you.
¹⁷ Show me your favor full and free
that my foes will be shamed and see,
　　　that you've cared and brought me through.

---

¹³⁵ Lit. "Unite my heart" means "let me focus solely on you without divided loyalties" or "Let my only concern be to worship you (fear your name)."
¹³⁶ Lit. "Lowest Sheol," "the place of the dead." David has been saved from the grave.
¹³⁷ Lit. "handmaiden." Interpreted generally to mean that David's mother was loyal to God, and so is he.

Psalm 87

A song. A psalm written by the descendants of Korah.

1-2 The LORD set his city Zion[138]
 on a hill, holy and high.
In all Israel, he loves her most —
 the apple of his eye.
3 O city of God, what's said about you,
 are things that magnify.　　　　　　*Pause and reflect*

4 God says:
 "I'll record Babylon and Rahab
　　as those who've come to know me.
 I'll add Tyre, Philistia, and Cush.[139]
　　Some there have bent the knee.
And I'll say:
 THESE ONES ARE MINE,
 BORN IN ZION."

5 The Most High himself will strengthen her way.
When people speak of Zion, they'll say:
 "This one is his.
 That one is his."
　　"YES, THEY ARE MINE,
　　BORN IN ZION."

---

[138] This psalm is a song of Zion, meaning Jerusalem. Zion is set on a mountain (hill) among other mountains in the area (v 1). "apple of his eye" is not in the Hebrew, but it is a metaphor used elsewhere to show God's love for Zion. "Bending the knee" is added to v 4 but is not in the Hebrew text. The Hebrew has "one is born there" or slight variations of that (vv 4, 5, and 6) but this clearly refers to "Born in Zion," a recurring theme in the poem. Vv 3-6 focus on a future look at the heavenly Zion, that is, being a citizen of God's kingdom. In this way, Zion is considered to be the "city of God" (v 3) or the mother city of all nations (see Isaiah 2:2-4, 26:1-2, 60:14-22, 61:1-7). Paul refers to this idea in Gal 4:26 that Jerusalem (Zion) is "above" and "our mother." For a good exposition of this poem see W. A. vanGemeren's analysis in the *Expositor's Bible Commentary*.
[139] These five nations represent five main enemies of Israel. Rahab refers to Egypt. Cush may refer to the upper Nile region (Nubia), Ethiopia, or Sudan. Even among God's enemies, there are those who are his children, part of his kingdom.

⁶ The LORD will make a list
of his people, he'll insist:
"EACH ONE IS MINE,
BORN IN ZION." *Pause and reflect*

⁷ Singers and dancers will say what's true:
"The source of our life is in you."

Psalm 88

A psalm written by the descendants of Korah. For the music director.
To be sung to the tune "The Suffering of Affliction."
A contemplative song written involving Heman the Ezrahite.

¹⁻² O LORD, my Savior, my words rise ...
day to night to day to ...
hear my plea, O God, to you.
PRAYER CRIES.[140]

³ Deep troubles appear,
death draws near.
⁴⁻⁵ Like a dead man am I,
forsaken to die.
Weakened warrior,
corpse in a grave,
forgotten, none can save.

⁶ In depths of darkness I sit ...
placed there by you in this pit.
⁷ From your waves of anger I reel,
crushing heaviness I feel. *Pause and reflect*

---

[140] This overall theme of "cries of prayer" is underlined in this psalm (vv 1-2, 9, 13). Keep in mind that the psalmist is being totally vulnerable in this psalm, expressing feelings of desperation in a hopeless situation. The personal expression of confidence or trust in the LORD is only implied, but the psalmist is continually praying to God! The seeming lack of overt trust and pervading outward expression of hopelessness in the psalm is why some scholars call Psalm 88 "the darkest of the lament psalms" or "the saddest of the Psalms" (Tate, *WORD Biblical Commentary*).

⁸ Loathed and chased away
 by closest friends.
You've caused this. ... Entrapped, no escape, ...
 to what ends?

⁹ Anguished suffering, ... my eyes.
 Hour to hour to ...
 hands lifted to you ...
PRAYER CRIES.

¹⁰ **Miracles for the dead ... do you do?**
Do they rise to praise you?   *Pause and reflect*
  ¹¹ Your loyal love declared,
  your faithful ways blared ...
   from the grave?
    ¹² Your right acts ... in a forgotten land known?
    Your wonders ... in darkness shown?

¹³ Each morning
 when I rise
to you, LORD ...
 PRAYER CRIES.

¹⁴ Why do you turn away ...
and **reject?** ... I feel gray.¹⁴¹
  ¹⁵ Sickness ... no breath,
  afflictions, near death,
   since I was young,
  from your attacks I've borne.
   I'm unstrung.

¹⁶ Your rage has rushed on me.
Terrors crushed on me.
  ¹⁷ All day flood-like they surround me.
  They engulf me, astound me.

---

¹⁴¹ The literal idea here is a deep sense of abandonment from God's presence.

¹⁸ Friends, loved ones abandon,
 I'm at an end. ...
    Darkness ...
 my closest friend.

Psalm 89

  A contemplative song written by Ethan the Ezrahite.

¹ O LORD, I'll sing of your loyal love.
 Forever it will be my song.
I'll tell your truth to each generation.
  ² I'll proclaim it my whole life long:
   Steadfast forever is your loyal love.
   Your truth's established in heaven above.

³ You said, "I've sworn an oath to David,
 my chosen one who serves me.
⁴ For each generation I'll give you
 a royal line, ... endlessly."   *Pause and reflect*

⁵ LORD, the gathered holy ones in heaven,
 praise your truth and wonders outpoured.
⁶ For who among the beings above
 can be likened to the LORD?
⁷⁻⁸ In the council of the holy ones
 our faithful God is revered.
He's the LORD God who rules over all.
 No one's more admired or feared.

⁹⁻¹⁰ You have crushed the sea monster Rahab,
 with power you've scattered your foes.
You rule over majestic oceans.
 You make the waves repose.
¹¹ You made the world and all it contains.
 The earth and sky belong to you.
¹² The north, the south, Mount Tabor and Hermon,
 to you their praises break through.

¹³⁻¹⁴ Your throne is based on justice and fairness.
  You're powerful and strong.
You lead the way with truth and great love
  which lead to a victory song.

¹⁵ Favored are those, LORD, who worship you,
  who live with you in your light.
¹⁶ They rejoice in you throughout the day,
  for you do what's good and right.
¹⁷⁻¹⁸ Our king, our shield, belongs to the LORD,
  to Israel's Holy One.
Our king, the people's splendor and strength,
  wields power second to none.
¹⁹ To your own you once spoke through a vision,
  a selecting work you had done.
You've raised up a helper, a warrior,
  from the people, a chosen one.

²⁰ You said: "I've poured oil on my servant.
  I've anointed David as king.
²¹ I'll steadfastly strengthen and uphold him.
  To him great power I'll bring.
²² No wicked person or enemy
  will overwhelm or defeat him.
²³ Those who hate him, yes all his foes,
  I'll crush and unseat them.

²⁴⁻²⁶ I'll extend his rule over the sea.
  Hostile kingdoms he will claim.[142]
My loyal love and truth will be with him.
  He'll win battles in my name.[143]
'My Father, my Rock, my Savior, my God,'
  about me he'll proclaim.

---

[142] The "sea" and "rivers" in the Hebrew text are most likely symbols of hostile powers that oppose.
[143] "Horn" in the Hebrew text is probably here used as a metaphor for military strength – "horn of an ox" is the referent.

27 He's my firstborn, the highest of earth's kings,
      my chosen whom I commend.
28 I've secured my fixed promise with him.
      I'll show him my love without end.
29 His dynasty will always endure,
      through those who from him descend.

30-31 But if his children forsake my teaching,
      and violate my demands,
if they don't uphold my justice,
      and won't obey my commands,
32 then I'll punish their sins with correction,
      they'll suffer at my hands.
33 But I'll never stop loving David.
      My faithfulness will move ahead.
34 I won't break my fixed promise to him,
      nor change what I have said.
35 I've sworn to him by my holy name.
      It's final, I cannot lie.
36 His dynasty will always continue
      like the sun abides in the sky.
37 Just like the moon it will endure,
      as a true witness on high."   *Pause and reflect*

38 But you're angry, God, with your chosen king.
      You've despised him who was "crowned."
39 You've broken your covenant with him,
      and cast him to the ground.
40 You've torn down all his city walls,
      and knocked his towers down.

41 All who pass by are stealing from him.
      His neighbors reproach and berate.

⁴² You've allowed his foes to win over him.
>They rise to celebrate.
⁴³ You've not upheld him in battle,
>but have forced him to retreat.

⁴⁴ You've ended the splendor of his crown,
>and made him obsolete.
⁴⁵ You've shortened the years of his youth,
>and shamed him, brought him defeat. *Pause and reflect*

⁴⁶ How long, LORD? Will you always hide yourself?
>Will your wrath keep burning like fire?
⁴⁷ You know how fleeting and short is my life.
>Our lives seem futile and dire.
⁴⁸ None can keep living and not pass away.
>We're destined to expire.   *Pause and reflect*

⁴⁹ Where Lord, is your loyal love for David?
>Where's the faithful oath you swore.
⁵⁰ See Lord, how all nations reproach us,
>and all the taunts they outpour.
⁵¹ Your foes, LORD, scorn your chosen king.
>Each step he makes, they mock him more.

⁵² Praise the LORD forever.
>Let praises flow.
>Yes, may it be so.
Amen.

Book 4 (Psalms 90-106)

Psalm 90

A prayer written by Moses, the man of God.

¹ As time marches on, Lord,
    each generation,
        you have been our dwelling place.
² Before the mountains were born,
        or you formed earth's face,
    from beyond time's limits,
        eternally, you are God.

³ "Return to dust, O man," you say forthright,
    and they turn back to dust.
⁴ A thousand years in your sight
    are like a passing day,
like a few hours of night.[144]

5-6 You sweep men away like broom, like brush,
    whisked into a deathly sleep.
They rise like the morning grass, so lush, ...
    yet as they near dusk's dark deep,[145]
they wither and dry, lie crushed.

⁷ Your fierce anger against us terrifies.
⁸ Our sins, our secrets, set before your eyes.
    ⁹ Our woeful days pass
    under your wrath.
Our weary years finish with sighs.

¹⁰ Our lives are spent at seventy years,
    or eighty, if we're strong.
Yet their sole boast is angst and sorrow,
    off we fly before long!

---

[144] The literal text "watch of the night" refers to a three-hour time period.
[145] The simple Hebrew image of "the darkness of evening coming" is drawn out for poetic purposes.

¹¹ Your mighty anger, who knows it,
　　　　or the fear that's due to you?
¹² Each day teach us to measure well,
　　　　to be wise in all we do.

¹³ Come back to us, O LORD!
　　　　How long will you delay?
Shower fully your compassion
　　　　on your servants now we pray.
¹⁴ May your loyal love come fill us,
　　　　so we'll shout for joy each day.
¹⁵ Bring us corresponding joy
　　　　to the misery of our way.

¹⁶ May we, your servants, see your mighty deeds.
　　　　May our descendants see your glory.
¹⁷ May your favor, Lord God, rest on us,
and work through us, oh work through us, …
　　　　to succeed in our story.[146]

Psalm 91

¹ The dweller in the shelter of God Most High
is shielded in the shade of El Shaddai.[147]

² O LORD, you are my fortress,
　　　　you are my hiding place.
You are the God in whom I trust:
　　　　my abiding place.
³ He'll save you from the hunter's trap
　　　　and lethal pestilence.
⁴ His truth will be your sheltering shield,
　　　　his wings your strong defense.

---

[146] Lit. "establish the work of our hands." This is an idiom for succeeding as God works in and through us.

[147] In Hebrew *El Shaddai* is the full name but *Shaddai* is the Hebrew text here. It is often translated "the Almighty" but the full term was kept here for poetic and rhythmic reasons. It is a name associated with power, sovereignty and authority.

5 You'll have no terror in the night,
      no arrow strike by day,
6 no plague will smite, at noonday bright,
      no disease along your way.
7 A thousand drop beside you:
      Now don't be alarmed.
Ten thousand more around you,
      and you won't be harmed!
8 You'll look and see the wicked fall
      before your very eyes.
9 If you make the LORD your refuge,
      if he's your God Most High,
10 no evil will befall you
      no plague will come nearby.

11 For he'll give orders to his angels
      to watch fully over you
to protect you and guard you well
      in everything you do.
12 They'll carry you with outstretched hands,
      if you fall down or are thrown,
so that your feet will not become
      injured by a stone.
13 You will trample underfoot
      each lion and each snake.
Even a spitting cobra,
      you will crush and break.

14 "I'll save those who love me," God says,
      "and guard those who trust in me.
15 To me my people will call out.
      I'll answer them faithfully.[148]
I'll be with them in times of trouble,
      honor them, set them free.
16 I'll gladden them with a long, long life.
      My salvation they will see."

---

[148] "Faithfully" is not stated in the original text, but implied.

Psalm 92

A psalm. A song to be sung on the Sabbath day.

1 It's good to give thanks to you, LORD Most High,
    and sing praises to your name.
2 Morning and evening declaring your love,
    and your faithfulness just the same,
3 playing a harp and a ten-stringed guitar,
    raising sounds that proclaim.

4 Your actions, O LORD, they make me rejoice.
    I sing gladly of what you've done.
5 How marvelous are your works outpoured!
    How deeply your thoughts run!
6 A stupid person and a fool
    can't understand this way:
7 "Though the wicked seem to sprout like grass,
    they're erased for endless days."

8 O LORD, you are eternally
    in your place on high.
9 Wrongdoers will be scattered,
    and your foes will die.
10 You've made me as strong as a wild ox.
    You've poured on me pure oil.
11 I've heard and seen the fall of my foes,
    their tortured cries, turmoil.
12 The just ones will spread and rise like cedars.[149]
    They'll prosper like a palm tree.
13 Rooted in our LORD God's house and courts,
    they will thrive full and free.
14 And when they grow old, they'll keep bearing fruit.
    They'll remain healthy and green.
15 They'll proclaim: "My Rock, the LORD, is righteous.
    No wrong in him is seen."

---

[149] Lit. "cedars of Lebanon".

Psalm 93

1 The LORD rules as king, he's majestic.
　　　　He's royally robed in might.
The world stands firm, established and sure.
　　　　It can't be moved from its site.
　　　　　　　2 Your throne was set up long ago to last.
　　　　　　　You're from beyond time: future and past.

3 The oceans raise their mighty voice, LORD.
　　　　Waves roar, thunder, and splash.
4 You LORD on high are so much more mighty
　　　　than waters' deafening crash.
　　　　　　　5 Your laws, LORD, stand firm without measure.
　　　　　　　Your house is holy forever.

Psalm 94

1 O LORD God of vengeance, avenge.
　　　　May your splendid justice gleam forth.
2 Rise, O God, pay back the proud ones,
　　　　you who are Judge of the earth.
3 How long LORD, how long will it be
　　　　that the wicked are filled with mirth?

4 These doers of wrong are boastful.
　　　　Proud words from their trumpets are blown.
5 They pulverize, LORD, your people,
　　　　and afflict severely your own.
6 They kill the widow and stranger.
　　　　Orphans: They slay heartlessly.
7 They think Jacob's God won't notice.
　　　　They think the LORD cannot see.

8 Some of my people, they act like fools.
　　　　When will they learn and be wise?
9 Does he not hear, the Maker of ears?
　　　　And not see, the Former of eyes?

143

¹⁰ Does the Reprover of man not punish?
   Does the Teacher not teach man?
¹¹ He knows how our thoughts are senseless.
   He perceives our foolish plan.

¹²⁻¹³ Favored are those you reprove, LORD.
   You give them due rest from their woes.
Favored are those whom you give instruction.
   You entrap and destroy their foes.
¹⁴ The LORD won't abandon his people,
   those he chose to inherit.
¹⁵ Justice will be based on fairness again.
   The just will pursue its merit.

¹⁶ Who will stand against wrongdoers with me?
   ¹⁷ Without the LORD's help to save, …
I soon would have met my fate, it's clear,
   in the silence of the grave.
¹⁸ When my feet slipped, I cried to you, LORD,
   and your steadfast love held me up.
¹⁹ When doubts and worries poured through me,
   your comfort and joy filled my cup.

²⁰ Can destructive rulers your allies be –
   those who oppress with their laws?
²¹ They make plots against the innocent:
   death sentences made without cause.

²² But the LORD God is my Mighty rock.
   He's my Fortress, I'm safe within.
²³ He'll pay back my foes for their wickedness,
   and wipe them out for their sin.

Psalm 95
¹ Come, let's joyfully sing to the LORD.
   He's the rock of our salvation.
² Come into his presence and thank him
   with songs of celebration.

3 The LORD is the Great King over all gods.
4-5 The earth's depths are in his hand.
The mountain heights are his, and the seas.
He made them and sculpted the land.

6 Come, let's bow down and kneel in worship
before the LORD who made us.
7 For he's our God and we're his people,
a pasture's flock in his trust.

Listen today to his voice, don't rebel
8-10 like your fathers did at Massah.
There in the desert they tested me,
both there and at Meribah.
I was angry with them for forty years.
They were always going astray.
These people saw all the things I did,
but wouldn't obey my way.
11 So I swore an oath in rage, I expressed:
"Never, never ... will they enter my rest."

Psalm 96
1-2 Sing a new song[150] to the LORD.
Sing to him and praise his name.
Sing to the LORD, all people.
Each day his salvation proclaim.
3 Announce his great deeds among all nations.
Declare his glory and fame.

4 The LORD is great. Fear him over all gods.
He's worthy. Praise him who's on high.
5-6 Honor and majesty are in his presence.
Strength and light[151] in his temple lie.

---

[150] The "new song" is a response to the LORD, usually after some sort of deliverance. This could be a victory song in a war context. Some contexts, like this psalm, are more ambiguous.
[151] Lit. "splendor" or "glory."

All nations' gods are mere idols,
        but the LORD created the sky.

7 Laud the LORD's glorious strength, O nations!
        8 Praise his glorious name!
Come to his courts with an offering,
        and his honor acclaim!
            9 Worship the LORD in his holy splendor.
            O earth, shake before him in terror.

10 The world is firmly set, it won't budge.
        Tell all the nations that the LORD is king.
With fairness all peoples he'll judge.

11 Let the heavens rejoice, and the sea rip-roar,
        let the earth with gladness ring.
12 Let the fields and what's in them exult,
        let the forest sweetly sing.
13 Let all that exists rejoice in the LORD,
        for he comes to judge the world.
He'll judge rightly all its people,
        with his truth flag unfurled.[152]

Psalm 97

1 The LORD rules, let the earth rejoice.
        Let distant islands cheer loud.
2 He reigns with equitable justice.
        Around him dark clouds enshroud.
3 Fire burns before him, devouring his foes,
        to the left and right, all 'round.
4 His lightning flashes across the world.
        The earth shakes and fears, ... spellbound.
5 Like wax, mountains melt before him,
        before the Lord of the earth.
6 The heavens declare his justice.
        All see his glory burst forth.

---

[152] Lit. "He'll judge the world in righteousness and peoples with his truth."

7 Let all idolators be put to shame.
  All you gods: Kneel! Give him acclaim!

8 Zion and Judah hear the LORD's rulings,
  then they rejoice and applaud.
9 For you, LORD Most High, are above the earth,
  much higher than each god.

10 Those just ones who love the LORD,
  hate evil and all that's wrong.
He saves them from the wicked's power,
  and protects them all life long.
11 With the just and the upright ones,
  joy is found and light shines.
12 You righteous ones, praise the LORD's holy name.
  Rejoice in him at all times.

Psalm 98

A psalm.

1 Sing a new song[153] to the LORD,
  for he's worked in a wondrous way.
As our holy warrior,
  he's mightily saved the day.

2 The LORD has unveiled his power to save,
  revealed his just ways to nations.
3 Everywhere on earth it was seen,
  how our God has brought salvation.
    He was faithful to Israel, his own.
    His loyalty to them was shown.

4-5 All people, rejoice and sing to the LORD,
  break forth into joyful song.
Make melodious music to the LORD
  with the harp while you sing along.

---

[153] For "new song," see footnote for Ps 96:1-2. Ps 98 gives a description of the LORD as a mighty warrior who brings victory or deliverance. Thus, the translation "holy warrior" which is implied at the end of v 1.

⁶ Blow trumpets and a ram's horn as you sing.
    Shout joyfully to the LORD, the King.

⁷ Let land and sea and all life in them
    resound with a thunderous shout.
⁸ Let oceans rip-roar in applause.
    Let the hills as one sing out.
⁹ Let them sing in the LORD's presence,
    for he's coming to judge each person.
He'll judge justly all those on earth
    with fairness in right proportion.

Psalm 99

¹ The LORD rules – enthroned midst the cherubim.
    Let nations reverberate!
² The LORD is high above all peoples.
    He's revered in Zion as great.
³ Let them give thanks to your fearsome name.
    Holy is our Potentate.¹⁵⁴

⁴ O Powerful King, you love fairness.
    You've set in place equity.
In Israel you've done what's just and right.
    You're full of integrity.
      ⁵ To the LORD our God we lift up praise.
      Holy is he, our worship we raise.

⁶ Moses and Aaron were two of his priests.
    Samuel too sought him and prayed.
They all called out in the name of the LORD.
    He answered the prayers that they made.
⁷ He spoke to them in a pillar-like cloud.
    His laws and demands they obeyed.

---

¹⁵⁴ "God as Potentate" (all powerful), although true, is implied in the context but is not part of the Hebrew text here.

8 Our LORD God, you answered to Israel.
>>You showed you're a God who forgave.
But you're also a God who punished them,
>>for the evil ways they behaved.
>>>9 Worship at God's holy hill, give him laud.
>>>Bring praise to the holy LORD, our God.

Psalm 100

A psalm of thanksgiving.

1 Man, woman, child, ... the world,
shout with joy to the LORD!
>>2 Enter his presence with singing.
>>Serve him with glad hearts ringing.
>>>3 Acknowledge the LORD is God.
>>>>We're his people, the flock of his pasture.
>>>>We belong to him, made by the Master.
>>4 Come through his gates with thanksgiving.
>>>Enter his courts with praise.
Give praise to his matchless name
>>with grateful hearts ablaze.
5 The LORD is good.
>>His love is steadfast,
>>forever it will last.
Throughout each generation
>>his faithfulness holds fast.

Psalm 101

A psalm written by David.

1-2 I'll sing of your loyalty and justice,
>>and I'll live with integrity.
My music I'll direct to you, LORD.
>>When will you come help me?

In my own home I'll live constantly
>>with purity of heart.
3 I hate what's vile, detest the deceitful,
>>with them I'll have no part.
4 Perverse people will depart from me.
>>Evil I'll shun from the start.

149

5 Secret slanderers I will silence.
>   I won't put up with the proud.
6 I'll look for the faithful to dwell with,
>   only "just" servants allowed!
7 The deceitful won't live in my palace,
>   and liars won't stay in my sight.
8 I'll clear the land of the wicked each day,
>   and cleanse God's site from their blight.

Psalm 102

*The prayer of an afflicted and overwhelmed person
who pours out a complaint to the LORD.*

1-2 LORD, in this trouble I face, hear my prayer.
>   Listen to my earnest plea.
Don't turn away when I call for help.
>   Come now and answer me.

3-4 My body's inflamed like hot burning coals
>   without a need to be stoked.
I'm weary, can't eat, and withered like grass.
>   My days dissolve like smoke.
5-6 Like a jackdaw[155] am I in the desert.
>   My cries are just like their groans.
Like a small owl am I among ruins.
>   I'm nothing but skin and bones.
7 Like a lone bird am I on a rooftop,
>   as I lie restless and moan.

8 My foes insult me and curse my name.
>   All day they mock me with jeers.
9 I have ashes to eat as daily food.
>   My drink is mixed with my tears.

---

[155] A dark bird like a crow often found in the desert known for its piercing cries like "caw caw." Mostly seen in Eurasia and North Africa.

¹⁰⁻¹¹ My life is like long shadows at sunset.
  I wither like grass each day.
You've picked me up in your anger,
  and then threw me away.

¹² But you LORD, are a king forever.
  Your fame will always be known.
¹³ You arise to show mercy to Zion.
  Her favored time will be shown.
¹⁴ Your servants will pity her ruins,
  and cherish each of her stones.

¹⁵ Earth's kings will be awed at your splendor, LORD,
  and your name nations will fear.
¹⁶ For you, O LORD, will build up Zion,
  and you'll in your glory appear.
¹⁷ You'll hear the requests of those tossed aside,
  holding their prayers so dear.

¹⁸ Write down God's deeds for those after us,
  so they'll always praise the LORD.
¹⁹⁻²² When nations and kingdoms come together,
  and praise him as a vast horde.
They'll proclaim his name in Zion,
  and worship him as LORD.
For when he looked down on earth
  from his holy temple on high,
he heard the groans of captives,
  and those doomed to die.

²³ He dissolved my strength in the midst of life,
  and has shortened my fleeting days.
²⁴ I said, "Don't cut off my life while I'm young,
  you who endure always."

²⁵ The heavens and earth you made long ago.
      A work of art¹⁵⁶ you brought about.
²⁶ They'll come to an end, but you'll endure.
      like clothing they'll wear out.

You cast them off like old clothes,
      and they'll soon disappear.
²⁷ But you without change exist on and on,
      beyond time, without year.

²⁸ May our children dwell in your presence,
and grant safety for their descendants.

Psalm 103

Written by David.

¹ I PRAISE THE LORD
WITH HEART OUTPOURED.

I praise his holy name
      from the bottom of my heart.
² I praise the LORD, and I'll never forget
      the gracious gifts he imparts.

³ It's he who forgives all our sins,
      and heals all our sickness.
⁴ He crowns us with his kindness and love,
      and saves us from Death's bleakness.
⁵ He fills our lives, fulfills our desires
      with so many good things.
He renews our strength like new feathers
      that push forth on eagles' wings.

⁶ The LORD acts justly for all the oppressed,
      and he does what is right.
⁷ He revealed how he worked to Moses,
      and showed his people his might.

---

¹⁵⁶ Lit. "the work of your hands."

8 The LORD is merciful, gracious, patient,
   his loyal love's undeserved.
9 He won't stay angry forever,
   or hold his rage in reserve.
10 He won't repay us or deal with us
   as our sins deserve.

11 God's loyal love strengthens God-fearers,
   it's higher than the eye can see.
12 He's completely removed our sins from us,
   farther than east-west can be.

13 Like a father to children the LORD cares
   for those with awe-filled trust.
14 How we're formed he does not forget.
   He knows we're made from dust.
15 Human lives on earth are like grass,
   like wildflowers they grow.
16 But they perish and soon are forgotten,
   when hot winds start to blow.
17 The LORD's great love forever remains
   for those with awe-filled trust.
All their descendants will clearly know
   that he always does what's just.
18 For those who obey his covenant,
   and who do what his law says,
19 the LORD has set his throne above,
   he's king over all that is.

20 Praise the LORD, you mighty angels,
   who carry out God's commands.
21 Praise the LORD, you armies who serve him,
   who do his will and demands.
      22 Praise the LORD, you his creation,
      in each place of his dominion.

WITH HEART OUTPOURED
I PRAISE THE LORD.

Psalm 104

1-2 I praise you my LORD God, how great you are!
  You're royally robed in light.
You stretch forth the vast skies like a tent.
  You're glorious and bright.

3 On the sky dome's streams,
you lay house beams.
  The chariots are clouds you ride.
  On the wings of the wind you glide.
   4 Winds send your messages through,
   and flaming fire serves you.
5 The earth, you fixed firmly on foundations.
  It won't be moved, no one could.
6 The oceans, you covered like a robe.
  The waters, o'er mountains stood.
7 Your thunderous voice sounds, waters scatter.
  At your stern warning, they flee.
8 The mountains rise up, the valleys sink
  to where you've placed them to be.
9 A limit you've set that waters can't cross.
  Ne'er again such a flood to see.

10 You make springs gush forth into valleys,
  onward through mountains they burst.
11 They bring water to all of God's creatures.
  Wild donkeys quench their thirst.
12-13 You water mountains from your sky storerooms.
  The world sees your work, gladness rings.
The birds sing with cheer from nearby trees,
  from their place next to the springs.
14 You provide grass for cattle to eat,
  earth's plants and crops for our food,
15 oil for skin and bread to bring strength,
  wine to uplift our mood.

¹⁶⁻¹⁷ You GOD, made your trees: Lebanon's cedars.
  In them birds build their nests.
These cedars drink well, as do your¹⁵⁷ firs.
  There storks make homes of rest.
¹⁸ Wild goats find a home in tall mountains,
  rock badgers hide as bluffs' guests.

¹⁹ You created the moon to bring seasons.
  The sun sets just right in our sight.
²⁰ Darkness you placed so the wild beasts
  can prowl around at night.
²¹ Young lions look for the food you provide,
  stalking and roaring for prey.
²² They return, go to sleep in their dens
  at break of dawn each day.
²³ Then people go out and do their work,
  till evening they labor away.

²⁴ You LORD, made many works! They fill the earth.
  With wisdom you formed them all.
²⁵ The spacious ocean, with countless creatures,
  life astir – large and small.
²⁶ You made the sea monster to play in it,
  and men's ships sail through it all.

²⁷ They all rely on you to provide
  at just the right time their food.
²⁸ With your own hand you supply good things
  and give them in plenitude.
²⁹⁻³⁰ When you give them your breath, they're created.
  You bring life to earth so robust.
But if you remove your favor from them,
  they're frightened and non-plussed.
When you snuff out their breath of life, they die,
  and go back to the dust.

---

¹⁵⁷ "His" trees is implied for "firs" and is the interpretation for "cedars." Literally,
cedars are "trees of Yahweh" in this verse.

³¹ May the glory of the Lord always last.
        May he rejoice in what he makes.
³² At his touch the mountains pour out smoke,
        at his glance, the earth shakes.
                ³³ I'll always sing to you and give laud
                with my whole being, my Lord and God.

³⁴ May these prayer thoughts be pleasing to the Lord.
        I'll rejoice in him and adore.
³⁵ May sinners be destroyed on the earth,
        and the wicked exist no more.

I praise Lord with heart outpoured.
Hallelu-Yah, praise the Lord.

Psalm 105
¹ Give thanks to the Lord, call out to him.
        Tell the world what he has done.
² Sing praise songs to him, declare his deeds:
        the most wondrous works, bar none!
³ Let all who worship the Lord celebrate,
        and acclaim his holy name.
⁴ Seek the Lord's presence and strength always,
        let this ever be your aim.

⁵⁻⁶ O seed of Abraham, servants of God,
        O Jacob's seed, his chosen ones,
remember his marvels and fair judgments,
        and miracles he's done.
⁷ The Lord's judgments reach the whole wide world.
        He's our God for all our days.¹⁵⁸
⁸ He keeps his covenant forever,
        his word of promise always.

---

¹⁵⁸ "For all our days" is implied.

⁹⁻¹¹ To Abraham, Isaac and Jacob
　　　　he swore to give them Canaan.
He decreed it as an inheritance,
　　　　their own priceless possession.
To Israel he gave this covenant,
　　　　eternal, its succession.

¹² When just a few of **God's own** were there,
　　　　and strangers in all respects,
¹³ they wandered from country to country,
　　　　from one nation to the next.
¹⁴ But he wouldn't let any oppress them,
　　　　and warned kings on their behalf:
¹⁵ "Don't touch even one of my prophets,
　　　　or hurt my chosen staff."

¹⁶ God sent a famine to their country,
　　　　and deprived them of their food.
¹⁷ He sent Joseph on ahead of them,
　　　　sold into servitude.
¹⁸ An iron collar they placed on his neck.
　　　　They fettered his feet to bind him.
¹⁹ But one day his predictions came true,
　　　　and the LORD's process refined him.[159]
²⁰ Then Pharaoh sent him to be released.
　　　　The world's ruler set him free.
²¹⁻²² He put him in charge of what he owned,
　　　　to be one who ruled by decree.
Joseph led wisely **Pharaoh's house,**
　　　　teaching his leaders to see.

---

[159] The LORD tested him This was a refining of his faith (waiting for the LORD to accomplish his promise through Joseph's dreams).

²³ Then Israel¹⁶⁰ went to Egypt, "Ham's land,"
     and dwelt as strangers there.
²⁴ The LORD increased them more than their foes.
     They filled the land everywhere.
²⁵ He turned the Egyptians against his own
     to mistreat his servants there.
²⁶ God called his servants Moses and Aaron.
     He chose them and they were sent.
²⁷ They did his signs there among the people,
     and miracles as they went.
²⁸ He sent a darkness on Egypt's land
     for they'd cast God's words aside.
²⁹ He changed their rivers into blood,
     and all of their fish died.
³⁰ Frogs filled the land including the palace.
          ³¹ God spoke, and there swarmed gnats and flies.
³² He rained hail on them in their land,
     and flashed lightning in their skies.
³³ He ruined their vines and their fig trees,
     and broke down their trees in the land.
³⁴ Then he spoke, and hordes of locusts came,
     like a countless marauding band.
³⁵ Every green plant in the land they consumed.
     Their crops they came to destroy.
³⁶ He struck down all their firstborn sons,
     their first fruits, their pride and joy.

³⁷ The LORD brought them out with gold and silver,
     no one stumbled as they moved on.
³⁸ The Egyptians had dread of Israel,
     and rejoiced to see them gone.
³⁹ With a cloud God covered his people,
     and guided with fire by night.
⁴⁰ They asked – he sent quail and heaven's bread
     to help them in their plight.

---

¹⁶⁰ Israel and Jacob are used interchangeably in the original text here, but the overall result is that the nation of Israel multiplies in Egypt for God's purposes.

41 He split open a rock in the desert,
and waters gushed forth in their sight.

42 He did not forget his sacred promise
to Abraham his servant.
43 He led out his choice ones with gladness,
their shouts of joy were fervent.
44 They became heirs from others' labors,
whose lands he let them seize,
45 so they might obey all his teaching,
and observe all his decrees.

Let praise to him be outpoured.
Hallelu-Yah, praise the LORD.

Psalm 106
1 HALLELU-YAH, PRAISE THE LORD.
Let praise to him be outpoured.

Give thanks to the LORD
because he is good.
His love is steadfast,
forever it will last.
2 Who can praise the LORD enough for his acts,
his awesome deeds and might?
3 Favored are those who keep his just rulings,
who each time do what's right.

4 When you favor your own, LORD, think of me,
and show me your salvation.
5 Let me witness how you prosper them,
your chosen group and nation.
Let me rejoice with those, your heirs,
as they give exaltation.

⁶ Like our ancestors we've greatly sinned.
       We've been wicked and done what's wrong.
⁷ When in Egypt they dismissed your wonders,
       and forgot your love so strong.
They turned from you at the Red Sea.
       Rebellion was their song.

⁸⁻⁹ Yet you tongue-lashed that Sea and led them through,
       as though it were a desert zone.
You saved them to be true to your name
       to make your power known.
¹⁰ From Egypt's vast power you rescued them.
       You redeemed them from their foe.
¹¹ Their enemies drowned, and no one survived,
       when waters began to flow.
¹² Then your people believed your promises,
       and sang songs with praise aglow.

¹³ But they quickly forgot what you'd done, LORD,
       your counsel "to wait" they suppressed.
¹⁴ They lusted for food in the desert,
       and put you to the test.
¹⁵ So you gave them what they desired,
       plus a plague that oppressed.

¹⁶ The people grew jealous of Moses,
       and of Aaron, your holy priest.
¹⁷ The ground split open and swallowed Dathan,
       and Abiram's clan deceased.
¹⁸ Upon their followers a fire came down.
       Death on the wicked unleashed!

¹⁹ At Mount Sinai they fashioned a gold calf,
       and bowed to a mere idol.
²⁰ They replaced the glory of God
       for an earthbound-imaged bull!

21 You rescued them with great deeds in Egypt,
     but they forgot all about you.
22 You did wonders there at the Red Sea:
     awe-striking things to view.
23 You would have completely wiped them out,
     but for Moses your chosen one,
who stood in the way when you were enraged,
     so your judgment would not come.
24 They despised the desirable land,
     and did not trust what you promised.
25 They complained in their tents and disobeyed.
     Your voice they chose to resist.

26 So you solemnly swore an oath to them,
     that in the desert they'd perish,
27 and you'd scatter their children to nations,
     to live lives that were nightmarish.

28 Then your people worshipped Baal-Peor,
     ate offerings to gods who're dead.
29 They provoked your wrath by their actions,
     so a plague among them was spread.
30 But Phinehas rose and did boldly,
     and the plague was soon ended.
31 Now and for all generations,
     he will be commended.[161]
32-33 They enraged you LORD at Meribah's Spring.
     They rebelled against your Spirit.
Moses suffered from them when he rashly spoke. ...
     Your holiness: He did not fear it.[162]

34 You LORD told them to wipe out the nations,
     but they refused to obey.
35 Instead they mixed with the peoples,
     and copied their evil ways.

---

[161] Lit. "Credited to him as righteousness."
[162] This line is correct based on other texts but is not part of the original text here.

³⁶ They bowed to the idols of Canaan,
　　and this led them into a snare.
³⁷ Their own dear children they sacrificed
　　to demon spirits there!
³⁸⁻³⁹ They polluted the land with their bloodshed.
　　Their evil deeds made them defiled.
To Canaan's idols they poured out blood,
　　blood from each innocent child.

⁴⁰ So your anger burned on your people.
　　You were disgusted with your own.
⁴¹ You handed them over to their foes,
　　rulers they could not dethrone.
⁴² Their foes abused them and ruled over them.
　　Their strong arm pushed them around.
⁴³ You saved them often but they were rebels,
　　and their sins brought them down.
⁴⁴ Yet you LORD observed them in peril.
　　You heard their cry of despair.
⁴⁵ You changed your mind about judgment,
　　something which would have been fair.[163]
You remembered your covenant with them,
　　and showed them your love and care.
⁴⁶ You caused those who had conquered them
　　to pity them, then and there.

⁴⁷ Bring us back from the nations, O LORD God.
　　Deliver us, please come through.
So we may lift thanks to your holy name,
　　to rejoice and praise you.
⁴⁸ Praise be to you, LORD God of Israel.
　　Let praise to you be outpoured.
Evermore all the people will say: "Amen!"
　　HALLELU-YAH, PRAISE THE LORD.

---

[163] This line is implied and fills out the verbal idea of God "relenting" (see Genesis 6:6) or "changing his mind" (see Ps 110:4) which is the same verb in Hebrew.

Book 5 (Psalms 107-150)

Psalm 107

1-3 The LORD's redeemed, may they declare,
　　　those redeemed from mighty foes,
those he brought back from foreign countries,
　　　from wherever the wind blows ...[164]
　　　　may they declare these words:
　　　　　　"Give thanks to the LORD
　　　　　　because he is good.
　　　　　　　His love is steadfast,
　　　　　　　forever it will last."

4 Some meandered in the wilderness,
　　　far from the populous way.
5 They hungered and thirsted, losing hope,
　　　as their lives slipped away.
6 They prayed to the LORD in their distress,
　　　and he rescued them from their plight.
7 He directed them along their path
　　　to find a dwelling site.
8 Let them thank GOD for his love for mankind,
　　　and all the marvels he brings.
9 For he fills the hungry and thirsty,
　　　and graces them with good things.

10 Some lived in deep dark valleys of gloom,
　　　with chains in prison they were bound,
11 for they despised the Most High's counsel,
　　　and turned from his words so profound.
12 He humbled them with great suffering.
　　　They fell with no help around.

---

[164] "Wherever the wind blows" – Lit. "from east, west, north, and the sea." The "sea" is normally translated "south" following the Syriac.

¹³ They prayed to the LORD in their distress,
   and he saved them from their plight.
¹⁴ He rescued them out of gloom and darkness,
   and snapped their chains with might.
¹⁵ Let them thank GOD for his love for mankind,
   and all the marvels he brings.
¹⁶ For though trapped by steel bars[165] and bronze gates,
   he smashed all binding things.

¹⁷ Some acted like fools through rebellion,
   and suffered for their sin.
¹⁸ They lost their taste for all kinds of food,
   near death and in a tailspin.
¹⁹ In their distress they prayed to the LORD,
   and he rescued them from their plight.
²⁰ He sent out his message and healed them,
   and saved them from Death's might.
²¹ Let them thank GOD for his love for mankind,
   and all the marvels he brings.
²² Let them offer their gifts with thankful joy,
   declare his works and sing.

²³ Some set sail in ships on the strong sea
   to buy and sell their wares.
²⁴ They witnessed the LORD's work on waters,
   his wonders far beyond theirs.
²⁵ He spoke and assigned great winds to blow.
   A storm surge lifted waves high.
²⁶ The ship rose and fell in the turmoil.
   Their courage shrank by and by.
²⁷ As they staggered about like drunkards,
   all their skills were vain to apply.
²⁸ In their distress they prayed to the LORD,
   and he rescued them from their plight.

---

[165] Lit. "iron bars." Steel is formed from iron and is more rhythmic for this text. Researchers believe that steel artifacts can be dated to 1800 BC, well before all the psalms were written (according to traditional dates)!

²⁹ He calmed the storm and the waves became still,
      and returned all things upright.[166]
³⁰ So they rejoiced when the waves grew quiet
      as they reached their desired site.
³¹ Let them thank GOD for his love for mankind,
      and all the marvels he brings.
³² Let the leaders and all the assembly
      laud him with praise that rings.

³³ God turns rivers into desert places,
      springs into dry lands – works that stun,[167]
³⁴ fertile land into wasteland spaces
      because of wickedness done.
³⁵ But he turns deserts into bustling streams,
      dry land into springs that swell.
³⁶ He brings the hungry to settle there,
      to make a city to dwell.
³⁷ They plant fields and vineyards that have great yields.
      Their abundance does not cease.
³⁸ He blessed them to have many children,
      and their herds greatly increased.
³⁹ But when they decreased and were humbled,
      by trouble, sorrow and pain,
⁴⁰ he made their oppressors roam trackless lands,
      showing these foes his disdain.
⁴¹ He rescued the needy from misery,
      and their families grew like flocks.
⁴² The godly will see and have joy,
      the wicked are hushed with shock.

⁴³ Let the wise watch these things and not ignore.
Let them ponder the great love of the LORD.

---

[166] This line is not in the Hebrew text, but it can be implied.
[167] "Works that stun" is implied from the context of the psalm but is not specifically mentioned in the Hebrew for this verse.

Psalm 108

A song. A psalm written by David.

¹ All my thoughts, O God, are firmly fixed,
    with all I am I'll sing and praise.
² Wake up, O drum! Rise quickly, O harp![168]
    I'll waken the dawn's first rays.
³ I'll thank you among the peoples, O LORD!
    Among the nations I'll praise you.
⁴ Your faithfulness is higher than the sky.
        Your love goes beyond our view.
            ⁵ May praise be raised, O God, far above the sky.
            Yes, throughout the world, may your glory fly.[169]

⁶ Answer my prayer to save your loved ones.
        Yes, rescue them by your power.
⁷ God has uttered from his holy place:
    "I'll triumph in this hour.
Shechem, Succoth, ⁸ Gilead, Manasseh,
    they all belong to me.
Ephraim will provide my warriors,[170]
        Judah, my royalty.[171]
⁹ Moab will I use to wash my feet,[172]
        and Edom belongs to me.[173]
The Philistines I will soundly defeat,
    and shout in victory."

¹⁰ Who'll take me to the armed and walled city?
        Who'll direct my way to Edom?
¹¹ Have you renounced us and our armies, o God, ...
        not with us in war to freedom?[174]

---

[168] Lit. "the lyre and harp" here.

[169] Lit. "May your glory be above all the earth." or "upon the earth."

[170] Lit. "the helmet of my head."

[171] Lit. "my scepter." A symbol of a ruling king.

[172] Lit. "a pot of my washing" or "wash basin" meaning it is completely subdued and held in contempt.

[173] Lit. "toss my sandal over" which is a symbol of ownership.

[174] Lit. "not going forth with our armies (in battle)."

¹² Grant us help from those warring with us,
>   for human help is all vain.
¹³ God will tread on our enemies.
>   With him the conquest we'll gain.

Psalm 109

For the music director. A psalm written by David.
¹ My God, you are my praise, don't be silent.
>   ²⁻³ People accuse me without cause.
Wicked liars raid me with hateful speech,
>   with slanderous lies from their jaws.
⁴ They pay back my love by accusing me,
>   but I'll respond with prayer.
⁵ They pay me back evil for my good deeds,
>   and hatred for love I share.

⁶ Choose someone wicked against my foe.
>   May someone stand and accuse him.
⁷ May he stand trial and be found guilty.
>   May his prayer be counted as sin.
⁸ May someone else take his position.
>   May his time be brief in this life.
⁹ May his children become lonely orphans.
>   Make a widow of his wife.
¹⁰ May his children be chased from their "ruins."¹⁷⁵
>   Make them roam and beg in their strife.

¹¹ May creditors seize what belongs to him.
>   May strangers loot all he owns.
¹² May no one care for his orphaned children.
>   May kindness to him not be shown.

---

¹⁷⁵ The Hebrew text says "seek." The Greek text says "driven" or "chased." "Ruins" refers to run down habitations.

¹³ May his family name be wholly wiped out.
        May all his descendants die.
¹⁴ May the LORD remember the guiltiness
        of his ancestors gone awry.¹⁷⁶
¹⁵ May the LORD recall these sins forever,
        and thoughts of him sputter and die.

¹⁶ For he did not think beyond himself,¹⁷⁷
        refusing to be kind.
The poor and needy and disheartened,
        he vexed, killed, and maligned.
¹⁷ He loved to curse and refused to bless.
        May his curse bounce back and bind.
¹⁸ He clothed himself completely in cursing.
        May his curse go down deep and spoil,
penetrating his being like water,
        and all his bones like oil.
¹⁹ May his curse wrap around him like clothes,
        or a belt around his waist.
²⁰ Like this may the LORD avenge my foes,
        those who accuse and lambaste.

²¹ But your love, Yahweh my Lord, is loyal.
        Help and save me for your name's sake.
²² I'm poor and needy and deep within ...
        my pierced heart's about to break.
²³ I'm cast away like a mere locust,
        fading like an evening shadow.
²⁴ I'm weak from fasting, just skin and bones.
        My weight's abysmally low.
²⁵ People scorn me, joke about me, see me, ...
        and shake their heads to and fro.

---

¹⁷⁶ The Hebrew text speaks of the "guilt of his fathers" and "sin of his mother."
These ideas are combined here.
¹⁷⁷ "Not thinking beyond himself" is clearly implied, but not part of the Hebrew
text.

²⁶ Help me, Yahweh my God, deliver me
　　　 because of your loyal love.
²⁷ My foes will see what you've done for me,
　　　 strengthening me from above.
²⁸⁻²⁹ May those attacking me be clothed with shame.
　　　 They may curse me, but you'll bless me.
Their disgrace will wrap them like a robe,
　　　 but I'll be joyous and free.

³⁰ I'll praise the LORD among the people.
　　　 I'll thank him vociferously.
³¹ He helps those in need from accusers.
　　　 He lifts them victoriously.

Psalm 110

A psalm written by David.

¹ Revealed...¹⁷⁸ The LORD says to my Lord:
　　　 "Sit at my right-side seat,
until I make your enemies
　　　 a footstool for your feet."
² The LORD will stretch forth from Zion
　　　 your mighty scepter, and say:
"Rule over these your enemies,
　　　 and in their midst hold sway."
³ On the day in which you battle,
　　　 your young men will come to you,
arrayed in holy splendor
　　　 like the morning dew.

⁴ The LORD has sworn an oath,
　　　 and will not take it back.
You are a priest forever
　　　 just like Melchizedek.

---

¹⁷⁸ "Revealed" translates the Hebrew word for "utterance" of the LORD, common among the prophets of a revelation or clear message from the LORD. It is only used twice in the Psalms (here and Ps 36:1 where it is translated differently).

5-6 On the day of the Lord's wrath,
      with him as your whelming force,
he'll judge all nations, crush world's kings,
      fill the land with corpse on corpse.
          7 This priest will drink from a brook on the way.
          With head held high he'll win the day.

Psalm 111

1 Hallelu-Yah, praise the LORD!
Let praise to him be outpoured.

א **(Aleph)**	I will thank the LORD with all my heart
ב **(Beth)**	in the gathered group of those set apart.
ג **(Gimel)**	2 Magnificent are the LORD's deeds,
ד **(Daleth)**	studied by those who enjoy them.
ו **(Waw)**	3 His righteousness stands forever,
ה **(He)**	his works are a dazzling gem.[179]
ז **(Zayin)**	4 His great wonders are to be thought about.
ח **(Heth)**	He's full of grace and kind.
י **(Yodh)**	5 He always remembers his promises.
ט **(Teth)**	He gives to his faithful on time.[180]
כ **(Kaph)**	6 His people were shown his mighty works.
ל **(Lamedh)**	Others' lands they gained for free.
מ **(Mem)**	7 Each thing he does he is faithful and fair:
נ **(Nun)**	reliable, each decree.
ע **(Ayin)**	8 In every way they are true and right,
ס **(Samekh)**	and will last for eternity.[181]

---

[179] Lit. "his splendor and majesty." Also, the lines *he* and *waw* were reversed here for poetic reasons.

[180] The lines *teth* and *yodh* were reversed for poetic reasons.

[181] The lines *samekh* and *ayin* were reversed for poetic reasons.

פ **(Pe)**	9 He redeemed his people, setting them free.
צ **(Tsadhe)**	His covenant will endure endlessly.
ק **(Qoph)**	Holy and fearsome is he.

ר **(Resh)**	10 Wisdom starts with the LORD's fear each day.
שׁ/שׂ **(Sin/Shin)**	Obey his decrees, you'll know his ways.
ת **(Taw)**	Ever and ever to him be praise.

Psalm 112

1 Hallelu-Yah, praise the LORD!
Let praise to him be outpoured.

א **(Aleph)**	Favored[182] is he who respects the LORD,
ב **(Beth)**	rejoicing in his commands.
ג **(Gimel)**	2 His godly seed will be strong on the earth,
ד **(Dalet**	his offspring blessed in the land.
ה **(He)**	3 Riches and wealth reside in his house.
ו **(Waw)**	His right acts forever endure.
ז **(Zayin)**	4 The light of the upright shines in the dark.
ח **(Heth)**	His grace, kindness, mercy are sure.

ט **(Teth)**	5 Good comes to him who gives freely.
י **(Yodh)**	Integrity rules all his ways.
כ **(Kaph)**	6 The righteous won't ever be shaken.
ל **(Lamedh)**	They're honored for endless days.

מ **(Mem)**	7 He has no fear to face bad news.
נ **(Nun)**	Unswerving, his faith in GOD shows.
ס **(Samekh)**	8 His resolve firmly fixed without fear.
ע **(Ayin)**	He'll trample all of his foes.
פ **(Pe)**	9 Freely he shares with the needy.
צ **(Tsadhe)**	His right acts will be commended.

---

[182] In this acrostic psalm vv 5 and 6 are highlighted to show the center of the poem. I've indented it and put in blank lines around these two verses to show its importance. Verse 1 introduces the poem with wisdom notions of "fearing the LORD" and "delighting in his word." The wicked are contrasted in v 10 with the three Hebrew letters that begin each line spelling רֶשֶׁת *reshet* which means a "net" or "snare." This hidden message seems intentional by the author.

ק **(Qoph)**   Blow loudly the trumpet to laud him.
                His honor won't be ended.
ר **(Resh)**   10 Wicked ones will see, be offended.
שׂ/שׁ **(Sin/Shin)** Great anguish is theirs, they'll fade away.
ת **(Taw)**   Their hopes forever upended.

Psalm 113

1 HALLELU-YAH, PRAISE THE LORD,[183]
    all you servants, praise and adore.
2-3 From east to west, and north to south,
    let praise to the LORD outpour.
Throughout the world,[184] praise now his name.
    Yes now, and evermore.

4 The LORD is high over all nations,
    his glory transcends the sky.
5 Who can compare to the LORD our God,
    who rules from his throne on high?
6 Who is like him who bends and looks down
    upon the earth and sky?

7 The poor he lifts up from the dust.
    He hoists them from their upheaval –
8 to seat them well with noble ones,
    the nobles of the people.

9 To the barren wife without progeny
God gives her a family.
    She's happy with his reward.
    HALLELU-YAH, PRAISE THE LORD!

---

[183] Pss 113-118 are traditionally read or sung during Passover and often at other feasts.

[184] The Hebrew text is from "sunrise to sunset" which has the meaning of each direction or in every place in the world.

Psalm 114

1 When God brought Israel out of Egypt,
    from that strange foreign land.
2 Israel became his holy dwelling,
    a kingdom in his hand.

3 The sea looked to flee
        and said, "Let's go!"
    and Jordan stopped its flow.
            4 The mountains skipped like rams,
            the hills, like lambs.

5 Why is it, sea that you flee and go?
O Jordan, that you won't flow?
        6 O mountains, skipping like rams?
        O hills, like lambs?

7 Tremble, O earth, at the Lord's presence,
    as the God of Jacob is near.
8 From rock, he makes waters flow.
    From flint, fresh springs appear.

Psalm 115

1 All glory be yours, LORD, not ours, not ours,
    because of your truth and love.
2 Why should nations ask: "Where is your God"?
        3 He does what he wants from above.

4 The idols of men are silver and gold,
    crafted with care by their hands.
5-7 They have throats but can't even mutter,
    they cannot understand.
They cannot smell or walk or feel,
    though there's a nose, feet, and hands.
They have mouths, they have eyes and ears,
    but can't speak, see, or hear.
8 Those who make them, and all who trust them
    become like them: fused atmosphere.

⁹ The LORD is your helper and shield.
    Trust him, O Israelites.
¹⁰ The LORD is your helper and shield.
    Trust him, O Aaronites.
¹¹ The LORD is your helper and shield.
    Trust him, those who fear him aright.¹⁸⁵
¹² The LORD will remember us and bless us:
    each Aaronite, each Israelite.
¹³ He will bless those who fear him:
    the small and great in his sight.

¹⁴ May the LORD enrich your lives fully,
    you and your children likewise.
¹⁵ May you all be blessed by the LORD,
    the Maker of earth and skies.

¹⁶ Heaven in its fullness is the LORD's.
    He gave earth to the human race.
¹⁷ Those who are dead can't praise the LORD,
    they descend to a silent place.
        ¹⁸ But we, the living, will give him praise,
        both now and always.

Let praise to him be outpoured.
Hallelu-Yah, praise the LORD!

Psalm 116

¹ I love the LORD because he's heard me,
    he's attentive to my prayers.
² Every time I call upon him,
    I know he listens and cares.

³ Death's tentacles all around, distress near,
    anguish and trouble have found me.
⁴ But on Yahweh's name I called out in prayer:
    "Please come and set me free."

---

¹⁸⁵ Fearing him aright is to revere him and it includes a respectful fear of his power and authority over our lives.

5 The LORD is righteous and full of grace.
　　He had compassion on me.
6 The LORD protects the innocent one.
　　I was weak but he set me free.
7 O my soul, be at rest and at peace.
　　The LORD has poured blessings on me.

8 You LORD have saved me from tears and death,
　　and kept me from falling down.
9 I will walk with the LORD throughout this life
　　with his presence all around.
10 Though I've been oppressed to the utmost,
　　I'll keep on trusting in you.
11 "Each person tells lies," I hastily said,
　　but you see all from your view.[186]

12 What shall I give back to the LORD
　　for all the good he's done for me?
13 I'll call on the name of Yahweh, my God,
　　as I raise "the cup that sets free."[187]

14 All my vows to the LORD I'll complete
　　before the gathered, the upright.
15 The death of the LORD's faithful ones
　　is valued highly in his sight.
16 I'm your servant, LORD, like my mother was,
　　you broke my chains by your might.

17 I'll bring you an offering of thanks.
　　Yes, Yahweh's name I'll entreat.
18 All my vows I'll complete for the LORD
　　before his people who meet.
19 In the temple courts of Jerusalem,
　　near his royal seat.

---

[186] This line is not in the Hebrew text but is clearly implied.
[187] "The cup of salvation" is traditionally part of the Passover meal in age-old Jewish tradition (compare Matt 26:27).

I praise you LORD with heart outpoured.
Hallelu-Yah, praise the LORD!

Psalm 117

1 Praise Yahweh,[188] all nations,
>and all peoples whosoever.
2 His loyal love to us is mighty.
>His faithfulness lasts forever.

Let praise to him be outpoured.
Hallelu-Yah, praise the LORD.

Psalm 118

1 Thank the LORD for he is good,
>for his love is steadfast,
>forever it will last.
2 Let Israel now acclaim:
>His love is steadfast,
>forever it will last.
3 Let Aaron's house exclaim:
>His love is steadfast,
>forever it will last.
4 Let God-fearers proclaim:
>His love is steadfast,
>forever it will last.

5 When I faced troubles, I prayed to the LORD.
>He answered me and set me free.
6 The LORD's with me, I won't be afraid.
>Who is able to harm me?
7 The LORD's with me to help. So, I'll triumph
>over foes who alarm me.

---

[188] Here the poem starts with "Praise Yahweh" and ends with "Praise Yah." I've kept the difference in the translation.

⁸ It's better to rely on the LORD
        than to trust in mankind.
⁹ It's better to rely on the LORD
        than to trust in leaders refined.
¹⁰ Hostile nations were all around me,
        but in Yahweh's name I beat them.
¹¹ On each side they came to surround me,
        but in Yahweh's name I beat them.
¹² They surrounded me like angry bees,
but like burnt thorns I smoked them with ease.
        In Yahweh's name I beat them.

¹³ My foes attacked me and I nearly fell,
        but the LORD rescued me.
¹⁴ The LORD is my strength and song,
        he saved me, set me free.
¹⁵ The LORD's **right hand** is strong and conquers.
        The just shout in exultation.
¹⁶ The LORD's **right hand** is strong and conquers.
        His right hand brings exaltation.

¹⁷ I will not die, instead I'll live,
        and the LORD's **deeds** I'll testify.
¹⁸ The LORD has punished me greatly,
        but has not let me die.
¹⁹ Open the gates of the just for me.
        I'll enter to thank the LORD.
²⁰ This is the LORD's **gate** – where the just go in –
        to worship him who's adored.¹⁸⁹
²¹ You have answered me and delivered me,
        so I'll thank you, O LORD.

²² The stone the builders rejected outright
        has become the cornerstone.
²³ This is the LORD's **work**, plain in our sight,
        it's amazing what he's shown.

---

¹⁸⁹ This line is implied but not in the Hebrew text.

²⁴ This is the day that the LORD has made.
  Let's live it with a joyous tone.

  ²⁵ LORD, please deliver us, come quickly.
  LORD, please grant us victory.

²⁶ Blest is the one who comes in Yahweh's name.
We bless you from his house, his domain.
  ²⁷ Yahweh, the LORD, is our God
    who shines upon us his light.
  Tie the sacrifice with ropes
    to the altar's horns tight.¹⁹⁰

²⁸ You are my God. I thank you, applaud you.
You are my God. I laud you.

²⁹ Thank the LORD for he is good.
  His love is steadfast,
    forever it will last.

Psalm 119
א (Aleph)
¹ Favored are those who are blameless and true,
  who live by the LORD's teaching.
² Favored are those who keep orders too,
  who seek him with all their being.
³ They don't act wrongly to any degree,
  but fully live out his way.
⁴ You've given to us each decree,
  that we should wholly obey.
⁵ Oh that my ways were firmly the same,
  to obey all your demands.
⁶ Then I would never be put to shame,
  when I study all your commands.

---

¹⁹⁰ This verse is interpreted in various ways. The last two lines of this verse are based on the NET Bible's rendering. See their note for this verse, and arguments for this rendering. "tight" is implied, but not in the Hebrew text.

7 I'll thank you with an honest heart,
     as I learn the good you require.
8 I'll obey your demands, doing my part.
     Don't forsake me – that would be dire.

‎ב (Beth)

9 If young people live in step with your word,
     they'll stay pure through all life's demands.
10 I'll seek you with a heart all stirred,
     let me not leave your commands.
11 I've hidden your promises inward,
     so I won't sin against you.
12 I praise you, please teach me, O LORD,
     all your demands so true.
13 With my mouth I recite what you say,
     all things you require of me.
14 Your orders with delight I obey,
     more joy than all riches would be.
15 I ponder your decrees as a treasure,[191]
     and contemplate your way.
16 All your demands give such pleasure.
     I'll remember your word each day.

‎ג (Gimel)

17 While I am living deal well with me,[192]
     so I can obey your word.
18 Open my eyes so I can see
     your marvelous teaching I've heard.
19 I live here on earth without belonging.
     Don't hide your commands from me.
20 Deep yearning within sets me longing
     for your rulings constantly.

---

[191] "As a treasure" is implied in the context. It's not part of the Hebrew text.
[192] Or, "Deal well with me, so that I will live and obey your word."

21 You rebuke the proud who are under a curse,
　　　for from your demands they stray.
22 Rid me of their contempt so perverse.
　　　Your orders are what I obey.
23 Though rulers gather and mock your servant,
　　　I'll ponder well your demands.
24 Your orders bring joy, make me fervent.[193]
　　　They guide me in all life's plans.

ד (Daleth)

25 Revive my life by means of your word,
　　　for my death is now at hand.
26 When I told you of my ways, you heard.
　　　Teach me what you demand.
27 Help me to know what your decrees teach.
　　　I'll ponder your marvels at length.
28 My spirit sinks as I weep with grief.
　　　By means of your word give me strength.
29 From false-filled ways, lead me to flee.
　　　Give instruction, grant me favor.
30 I will do all you require of me:
　　　A faithful path I savor.
31 I cling to your orders with heart and hands.
　　　May I not be put to shame.
32 I run, LORD, to follow your commands.
　　　You've opened my mind to attain.

ה (He)

33 Teach me, O LORD, of things you demand,
　　　and I'll keep them unswervingly.
34 Your teachings – help me to understand.
　　　I'll obey them unceasingly.

---

[193] Since God's word brings such joy, they motivate the psalmist. So, "make me fervent" is possibly implied.

35 On the pathway of your commands, lead me.
       It's there I find great delight.
36 May all my thoughts on your orders be
       with greed-tinged gain not in sight.
37 Let me not gaze on things of no value.
       Give me life through your way.[194]
38 Perform your promise for me who serves you,
       so you can be feared each day.
39 Remove from me the reproach I dread,
       for good are the rulings you give.
40 How I desire the decrees you've said!
       By your righteousness, let me live!

ו (Waw)

41-42 I answer those who scorn me "in word."
       Your word's my trust unabated.
Show your great love to me, O LORD,
       your salvation, ... as you've stated.
43 Help me speak always your word so true,
       for I've hoped in what you require.
44 I obey your teachings all the way through,
       ever and ever my desire.
45 I live my life in liberty,
       for your decrees I've sought out.
46 I declare your orders to royalty.
       No shame in me is brought out.
47 I love and take a simple delight
       in all of your commands.
48 I cherish and respect[195] them day and night,[196]
       as I ponder your demands.

---

[194] Some Hebrew texts read "by your words" here.
[195] Lit. "lift up my palms."
[196] Either "day and night" or "constantly" is implied.

ז (Zayin)

49 Don't forget your promise to me,
    for it has given me hope.
50 When I'm suffering, it comforts, sets free.
    Through it you've thrown a life rope.
51 Ouch, the proud scorn me like hot arrows fired,[197]
    but I, from your teachings won't swerve.
52 I recall, LORD, what's long been required,
    and take comfort there as I serve.
53 Rage shakes me because of those who do wrong.
    They have forsaken your teaching.
54 Divine demands are the words of my song
    in each place my steps are reaching.
55 At night, O LORD, I remember your name,
    that I may follow your teaching.
56 This is my practice, always the same,
    to keep your decrees in each thing.

ח (Heth)

57 All your words, LORD, I've promised to do,
    for you are my choice, my share.
58 With my whole heart I am seeking you.
    As you've promised, show gracious care.
59 I've walked in your orders by which I stand,
    when I thought about my way.
60 I move quickly to follow each command.
    I move without delay.
61 Though wicked tie me with a bond that yanks,
    I won't forget your teaching.
62 I'll rise at midnight to give you thanks,
    for your rulings so pleasing.
63 I'm friends with all who fear God above,
    to all who obey his decrees.
64 O LORD, the earth's full of your great love.
    Teach me your demands, oh please!

---

[197] "Flaming arrows" in Scripture are often connected to anger, in this case words of anger, but the Hebrew text here is simply "mocked me to the extreme."

ט (Teth)

65 You have done good things for me, your servant,
　　in keeping with your word.
66 Teach me knowledge and discernment.
　　I believe your commands, O LORD.
67 Before I suffered, I went my own way,
　　now I follow your word.
68 You do good and you are good each day.
　　Teach me your demands, O LORD.
69 I keep your decrees with all my being,
　　though the proud taint me with lies.
70 Their haughty hearts are cold and unfeeling,
　　but it's your instruction I prize.
71 It did me good to suffer intensely,
　　so your demands I could learn.
72 Your plain teaching is more treasured for me
　　than millions that I could earn.

י (Yodh)

73 Grant me insight for learning your commands,
　　for your fingers have shaped me, LORD.
74 May God-fearers see me and clap their hands,
　　for I have hoped in your word.
75 You have chastened me in a just way,
　　because your rulings are true.
76 May your great love console me each day,
　　as you've promised to do.
77 Have compassion on me so I can live.
　　Your teaching is my delight.
78 May the proud be ashamed for lies they give.
　　I'll probe your decrees for insight.
79 May God-fearers who know all your orders
　　look at my example and see.
80 May I keep all your commands with ardor
　　that no shame may fall upon me.

כ (Kaph)

81 I long for you deeply to rescue me,
   and in your word, I have hope.
82 Worn out, I wait for your promise to me.
   Grant comfort, help me to cope.
83 Like a dried-up wineskin I'm shriveled up,
   but to your demands, I'm true.
84 How long must I wait and be held up?
   Judge soon those who pursue!
85-86 The proud dig pits to crush ... with claims unjust,[198]
   which is against your instruction.
Each command you give is worthy of trust.
   Help, liars seek my destruction!
87 They almost destroyed me utterly,
   but from your decrees I won't stray.
88 Because of your great love, protect me,
   so your orders I may obey.

ל (Lamedh)

89 O LORD, your word abides eternally.
   It is firmly fixed in the skies.
90 To our seed your faithfulness will be.
   The earth you've established likewise.
91 Today stand your rulings – they're so right,
   for all things exist to serve you.
92 Unless your teaching had been my delight,
   I'd be dead from sorrow, it's true!
93 Your decrees I won't ever forget,
   for by them you gave life to me.
94 I've searched your decrees, that's my mind-set.
   Come save me. I'm yours totally.
95 The wicked are hoping to kill me.
   I'll ponder your laws to live under.
96 Each thing has a limit or boundary.
   Your commands are full of wonder.

---

[198] "Claims unjust" means false claims without cause ... "against me" is implied.

מ (Mem)

97-98 O how I love your teaching and commands!
     I think on them constantly.
They make me wiser than enemy bands,
     for your words are ever with me.
99-100 I know more than my elders and teachers.
     for I ponder your orders each day.
I understand more than these leaders,
     for all your decrees I obey.
101-102 From your divine rulings I did not stray,
     for you've been my teacher, O LORD.
I've held back my feet from each evil way,
     so I may follow your word.
103 How pleasing ... your promises to me,
     sweeter than honey to my taste!
104 From your decrees I gain knowledge and see,
     so I hate each step falsely traced.

נ (Nun)

105 Your word is a lamp to my feet,
     a light for my pathway.
106 Your righteous rulings I will keep.
     I've sworn to it come what may.
107 Give me life, LORD, by means of your word,[199]
     for I've suffered terribly.
108 Accept my free gifts of praise, LORD,
     and your right rules, please teach me.
109-112 I am heir to your laws forever.
     They're a joy to comprehend.
I won't renounce your demands, ... no never!
     I'll obey them to the end.
Though danger is constantly before me,
     your teaching I will recall.
Though the wicked have set a trap for me,
     your decrees: I'll keep them all.

---

[199] This could be to strengthen because of weakness or to keep alive. "By means of" could be because of God's promises or what he has already said.

ס (Samekh)

¹¹³ I hate the disloyal, to God they won't yield,
      but I love your teaching, O LORD.
¹¹⁴ You are my place of safety, my shield.
      I yearn full of hope for your word.
¹¹⁵ Leave me, you who cause evil and strife,
      so I can obey God's commands.
¹¹⁶ Uphold me, God, by your promise of life.
      Keep my hopes from shame-sinking sands.
¹¹⁷ I'll respect your demands and obey.
      Support me so I can be saved.
¹¹⁸ You shun those who hate your demands, who stray,
      for they act as liars, depraved.
¹¹⁹ You dump the wicked like dross, you subdue.
      That's why I love your laws.
¹²⁰ I'm fearful and shudder before you.
      Your rules I hold in awe.

ע (Ayin)

¹²¹ In what's right and fair I've been fervent.
      Don't leave me to those who aggress me.
¹²² Assure good things to your servant.
      Don't let the proud oppress me.
¹²³⁻¹²⁴ Toward your servant act with great love.
      Teach me your demands with insight.
My tears pour out seeking help from above:
      your promise to make things right.
¹²⁵ I'm your servant, help me discern,
      and understand your laws.
¹²⁶ Act now, LORD, for your teaching I learn,
      has been broken without pause.
¹²⁷ That's why I love your commands each day,
      more than gold, more than pure treasure.
¹²⁸ That's why I hate each crooked way.
      Your right decrees are my measure.

פ (Pe)

129 Your laws bring wonder and insight,
     so I follow them sincerely.
130 Your words like an open door bring light,
     making untaught ones see clearly.
131 I pant after your commands ardently,
     commands that I'm eager to do.
132 Look at me and be gracious to me,
     as you do for those who love you.
133 Guide my footsteps as you have promised.
     Let sin not reign over me.
134 Save me from those who've crushed and demolished,
     that I may keep each decree.
135 Show favor to your servant, shine your face,
     and teach me what you demand.
136 My tears pour out like a flood apace,
     for your teaching's not kept in the land.

צ (Tsadhe)

137 LORD, all things that you require are right.
     You are always just and fair.
138 You've given laws that are just in your sight,
     they're faithful beyond compare.
139 Indignation and anger consume me,
     for my foes disregard your word.
140 Your words are proven, refined so purely,
     that I love them all, O LORD.
141 Though I'm miniscule and hated,
     I remember decrees from you.
142 Your justice is eternal, undated.
     Your teaching is always true.
143 Distress and anguish have come to me,
     but it's joy that your commands give.
144 Your laws are righteous eternally.
     Help me to know them and live.

ק (Qoph)

145 "Answer me LORD" is the cry of my heart,
    and I will observe your demands.
146 "Save me LORD" is the plea I impart.
    I'll do what your law commands.
147-148 I'll stay awake all the night through,
    to ponder promises heard.
Before dawn, I'll rise and seek help from you,
    to find fresh hope in your word.
149 Hear my prayer, your great love is far-reaching.
    By your justice, give life, O LORD.
150 Evil schemers, those far from your teaching,
    have approached me like a horde.[200]
151 But you, LORD, are near, on this I depend.
    All your commands are truth.
152 You've established your laws till time will end.
    I learned this in my youth.

ר (Resh)

153 Look upon my distress and deliver,
    for I've not ignored your teaching.
154 Fight my cause, my redeemer, life-giver,
    through your promise out-reaching.
155 Wicked people remain far from saved,
    for they don't pursue your demands.
156 Your compassion flows like a grace wave.
    Give me life by rules you command.
157 My oppressors and foes are multiplied,
    but from your law I've not turned.
158 I'm disgusted with faithless ones who've lied,
    it's your word that they have spurned.
159 Give me life by your love so loyal.
    Look how I love your decrees, LORD.
160 All your right rulings are eternal.
    There's nothing but truth in your word.

---

[200] "Like a horde" is added for dramatic effect and rhyme.

שׂ/שׁ (Sin/Shin)

¹⁶¹⁻¹⁶² Like one who finds treasure abundantly,
>I rejoice in the promise I've heard.
Though rulers unjustly oppress me,
>I revere greatly your word.
¹⁶³ Falsehood and lies, I hate and despise.
>but how I love your teaching.
¹⁶⁴ Each day seven times, my praise fills the skies,
>for your just rules so far-reaching.
¹⁶⁵ Those loving your teaching have great peace.
>Nothing can make them fall.
¹⁶⁶ My hope for rescue, LORD, will never cease,
>I keep your commands great and small.
¹⁶⁷ I'm thrilled beyond measure to keep your laws.
>They are fantastic to me.
¹⁶⁸ Your laws and decrees I've kept without pause,
>for I know all I do you see.

ת (Taw)

¹⁶⁹ Grant me insight from your word, O LORD,
>as my plea enters your view.
¹⁷⁰ Rescue me by your promised sure word,
>as my prayers come before you.
¹⁷¹ May praise pour from me from what I've heard,
>as you've taught me your demands.
¹⁷² May I sing about your promised word,
>for just are all your commands.
¹⁷³ May your mighty hand be there to help me.
>Your decrees I've chosen to do.
¹⁷⁴ Your deliverance, O LORD, I yearn to see.
>Your teaching makes joy rise anew.
¹⁷⁵ May I live so I can give you praise.
>May your just rules help me to stand.
¹⁷⁶ Find your lost servant, who like a sheep strays,
>for I won't forget your commands.

Psalm 120

A pilgrimage song.

¹ I called to the LORD when in trouble,
    and he answered my cry:
² "Save me from deceivers, O LORD,
    and those who constantly lie."

³ O liar, what punishment awaits you?
    What judgment of God unfolds?
⁴ A sharp retort from a warrior's arrows –
    arrows forged on hot coals!

⁵ Woe is me! I live with the godless
    like those from Meshech or Kedar.²⁰¹
⁶ I've lived far too long among those for whom
    just the thought of peace they abhor.
⁷ I'm a man of *shalom*²⁰²
    yet when I speak, they are for war.

Psalm 121

A pilgrimage song.

¹ As I raise my eyes to the hills
    from where does my help upspring?
² From the LORD of heaven and earth,
    Creator of everything.

³ The one who protects you won't sleep.
    He won't let you stumble and fall.
⁴ Israel's ever-watchful guard
    never slumbers or sleeps at all!

---

²⁰¹ Meshech and Kedar could be a merism to represent people who were ungodly enemies of Israel who surrounded Israel (from north to south).
²⁰² The Hebrew text says only "I *shalom*." *Shalom* is the Hebrew word for "peace," but is often borrowed into English, especially in Jewish settings. *Shalom* has a broad range of meaning including "wholeness," "soundness," "completeness," "safety" and "in harmonious relationship."

5 The LORD himself will protect you.
     He is the shade on your right.
6 The sun will not smite you by day,
     nor the moon strike you by night.

7 The LORD will protect you from all evil.
     He'll guard your life wherever.
8 He'll protect your movements to and fro,
     both now and forever.

Psalm 122

A pilgrimage song. Written by David.

1 It made me glad when others said,
     "Let's go to the house of the LORD."
2 O Jerusalem, I'm here at your gates
     with others in one accord.

3 Jerusalem is a well-built city
     that's joined as one in unity.[203]
4 All the tribes make their pilgrimage there,
     GOD's tribes in community.
Israel comes there to praise the LORD's name:
     an order from what the law states.
5 It's here where Israel's kings rule,
     to judge the people's fates.[204]
6 Please pray for peace for Jerusalem.[205]
     May those loving you rest secure.
7 May peace be there inside your walls.
     May your towers be safe and sure.

---

[203] Some translations take this more literally as describing the compact design of the city. See the NET Bible's note for this verse which favors a more abstract interpretation (see also GNB).

[204] Verse 5 is literally: "(For or Indeed) there thrones for judgment were placed, the thrones of the house of David."

[205] There is alliteration of the "sh" and "l" sound three times in this verse in Hebrew. The translation captures an alliteration of three p's to imitate an aspect of this triple alliteration.

⁸ For the sake of my people and friends,
    may Zion truly have peace.
⁹ For the sake of our LORD God's house,
    I pray your success will increase!

Psalm 123

A pilgrimage song.

¹ You sit on your heavenly throne,
    as I raise my eyes to you.
² We gaze at you like true servants who seek
    their master's nod anew.
Or like a servant girl who desires
    her mistress' nodding cue.
All of us need your favor, LORD God,
    so we raise our eyes to you.

³ Show us your favor, LORD, yes, your favor.
    We've endured such mocking and scorn.
⁴ The haughty and proud have looked down on us.
    Untold contempt we've borne.

Psalm 124

A pilgrimage song. Written by David.

¹ If the LORD had not been with us,
    let all of Israel say—
² if the LORD had not been with us,
    when foes swarmed us to slay,
³ They would have consumed us alive
    in their rage and fiery breath.
⁴ The water and floods would have drowned us,
    because of their roaring depth.
⁵ Yes, the consuming, raging waters
    would have swept us to our death.

⁶ The LORD has not let their teeth tear us,
    so praise his name with me.
⁷ We've escaped like a bird from a trap,
    the trap's broken, and we're set free.

⁸ Our help is in the name of the LORD,
      Creator of sky, land and sea.

Psalm 125

A pilgrimage song.

¹ Those who trust in the LORD are unshaken,
      they're like Mount Zion – fixed always.
² As the mountains surround Jerusalem
      in each direction you gaze,
the LORD surrounds and protects his people,
      now and for countless days.

³ He won't let sinners rule the just's land,
      or lead the just to do wrong.
⁴ O LORD, do good for those pure of heart,
      who are doing good all along.
⁵ But punish those on twisted paths,
      who rush into sin headstrong.

Upon Israel, may peace find a home.[206]
Yes, may she have *shalom*.

Psalm 126

A pilgrimage song.

¹ When the LORD turned the tide for Zion,[207]
      it was like a dream come true.
² Our homes were loud with laughter,
      as raucous joy broke through.
"The LORD's done awesome things for them."
      The people near us said.
³ The LORD's done awesome things for us,
      and our joy's widespread.

---

[206] This line of the poem is a wordier version of the Hebrew text but does not change the basic meaning. *Shalom* in Hebrew means "peace" but has a wide range of meaning depending on context. The final verse of this psalm in Hebrew is only "Peace be upon Israel." See also Ps 135:5 for a parallel text.

[207] Lit. "turned a turning" could be a reference to bringing back from captivity or can be a more general idiom like "turn the tide" or "restore the fortunes of" (see Job 42:10). Even the more general idea could refer to a return from captivity.

4 Keep turning the tide for us, O LORD,
    like streams in the desert flow.
5 Those who sow life with tears, reap joy –
    a bumper crop to show.
6 Those who weep as they go to the fields
    who've brought their seed to sow,
will return with songs of raucous joy
    with a harvest overflow.

Psalm 127

A pilgrimage song. Written by Solomon.

1 Unless the LORD builds the house,
    the builders' work is useless.
Unless the LORD keeps watch on the city,
    the night guards' watch is fruitless.
2 It's useless for you to rise up early,
    and labor late for food to eat,
since God provides for those he loves,
    even while they sleep.[208]

3 Sons[209] are an inheritance from the LORD,
    they're a reward from the Giver.
4 Sons born in one's youth are like arrows
    in a warrior's quiver.
5 How favored is the man with many sons.
    He won't be put to shame.
When accused in court by enemies,
    his sons will defend his name.

---

[208] Or a second interpretation: "he gives sleep to those he loves."
[209] This could be translated "children" as in some translations, but v 6 seems to indicate that sons are in mind. In the culture they would be able to more easily defend the father or the house.

Psalm 128

A pilgrimage song.

1-2 How favored are you who fear the LORD.
  Great blessings are yours each day.
You'll enjoy the fruit of your labor,
  as you follow his way.
3 Your wife will be like a vine that's fruitful
  in the house that you possess.
Your children will be in your dwelling
  like olive shoots that impress.
4 For those who revere and honor the LORD,
  that is how he will bless.

5-6 May the LORD bless you from Zion.
  May good come to Jerusalem.
May you see that happen throughout your life.
  May you see your grandkids, each one.

Upon Israel, may peace find a home.[210]
Yes, may she have *shalom.*

Psalm 129

A pilgrimage song.

1 "From youth, foes have greatly assailed me,"
  let all of Israel say—
2 "From youth, foes have greatly assailed me,
  but they've not won the day.
3 I'm like a field where foes plowed my back,
  and gouged me with furrows long.
4 But the LORD is just and has set me free
  from the wicked's cords so strong."

5 May all those enemies of Zion
  be thrust back and disgraced.
6 May they be like grass on a rooftop:
  sprouting, drying, erased,

---

[210] See footnote in Ps 125:5 for a long explanation of this same rendering.

⁷ which cannot load a harvester's arms,
>> or fill a reaper's hands.
⁸ May no passerby give them GOD's blessing,
>> or consecrate their plans.

Psalm 130

A pilgrimage song.

¹⁻² From deep waters, LORD, I cry for mercy.
>> Hear me and keep me alive.
³ If you, LORD, kept a logbook of sins,
>> who could ever survive?
⁴ But forgiveness is found in you,
>> so we fear you and thrive.

⁵ I wait for the LORD, with all my being,
>> and I trust in his word and wait.
⁶ I wait for the Lord more than watchmen wait ...
>> for dawn's slow embrace,
the night-long drawn-out wearisome wait ...²¹¹
>> for dawn's slow embrace.

⁷⁻⁸ O Israel, hope in the LORD who shows love,
>> for with him there's loyalty.
Yes, he'll fully redeem Israel.
>> From their sins he'll set them free.

Psalm 131

A pilgrimage song. Written by David.

¹⁻² Calm.
>> Be still, my soul, ...
>>> I'm resting fully on you, LORD.
Like a weaned child with its mother,
>> quiet and content am I.
>>> I'm resting fully on you.

---

²¹¹ This line is not in the Hebrew text. It is implied and is added for poetic effect.

No swelled head
    or high and mighty look.
No grasping to be great
    or moving beyond my sphere.
        I'm resting fully on you.

3 O Israel, hope in the LORD.
Now and evermore.

Psalm 132

A pilgrimage song.

1 LORD, **don't forget** David, and his hardships.
    2 how he made an oath to the LORD,
a vow to the Mighty God of Jacob –
    spoken of his own accord:
3-5 "O **Mighty** LORD God of Jacob,
    I **won't** let my sleep accrue,
or return to my home till I find
    a dwelling place for you."

6 We heard the ark was in Ephrathah.
    In Jaar's fields it was found.
7 **Let's** go now to his dwelling place.
    At his footstool we'll bow down.

    8 Rise up, LORD,
        you and your ark of might,
        and come to your resting site.

9 Clothe your priests with your righteousness,
    may your faithful joyfully sing.
10 Because of your servant David,
    don't reject your chosen king.

11 The LORD swore an oath to David,
    not retracting what he'd made known.
"I, the LORD, declare that I'll set
    a son of yours on the throne.

¹² And if your seed obeys my promise,
  and the teachings that I've shown,
then their sons too will always rule
  on your royal throne."

¹³ The LORD's chosen Zion, and desired it
  for his dwelling place.
¹⁴ He said, "This is always my resting site.
  Here's my desired space."
¹⁵ "With sustenance I'll surely bless her,
  yes, food for the needy I'll bring.
¹⁶ Her priests I'll clothe with salvation,
  her faithful will joyfully sing.
¹⁷ From David's line my Anointed will shine.
  I'll augment his force and fame.
¹⁸ A resplendent crown he will wear,
  and I'll clothe his foes in shame."

Psalm 133

A pilgrimage song. Written by David.

¹ Unity in community:
  How truly wondrous when the people of God
live as one in unity!

² Unity is like sacred oil
  poured on the priest's head, ...
   flowing down on Aaron's beard, ...
    oozing smoothly on his collar's robe, ...
     down, ...
   and all around.

³ Unity is like the dew of Hermon,
flowing down on Mount Zion.
  Yes, there the LORD
   is expressing his blessing,
   even life everlasting.

Psalm 134

A pilgrimage song.

1 All you who serve in the LORD's house at night,
    worship him with praising.
2 Pray together in his holy house.
    Praise him with hands raising.

3 May the LORD God, the Creator of all
Let his blessing on you – from Zion – fall.

Psalm 135

1-2 HALLELU-YAH, PRAISE THE LORD!
Let praise to him be outpoured.

Praise the LORD's name, you who assist
    in the temple courts of our God.
Praise him you who serve in the LORD's house.
    Yes, praise him, give him laud.
3-4 Praise the LORD for he is good.
    He's chosen Jacob as his own.
Sing praise to his name for it's beautiful.
    Israel is his alone.

5 The LORD is indeed very great.
    He's greater than all deities.
6 He does whatever he desires
    in the sky, land and seas.
7 He causes clouds to rise from earth's limits,
    brings lightning flashes with rain.
He reached deep and summoned the wind
    from storerooms preordained.

8 The LORD himself wiped out Egypt's firstborn –
    man plus beasts of all kinds.
9 God moved against Pharaoh and his subjects
    by doing great wonders and signs.
10 Many nations he forcefully wiped out,
and great kings were part of his rout:

¹¹ King Sihon, the Amorite,
  King Og, the Bashanite,
all kings among the Canaanites, ...
  he crushed them in each fight,[212]
   ¹² and gave their land away
    to Israel his people
  to inherit on that day.

¹³ Your renown, O LORD, through our line will last.
  Your name will endure always.
¹⁴ The LORD will bring justice and show mercy
  to his servants all their days.

¹⁵ The nations' idols are gold and silver,
  the works of human hands.
¹⁶⁻¹⁷ They have a body but no breath.[213]
  They cannot understand.[214]
They have mouths, eyes and ears,
  but can't speak, see or hear.
¹⁸ Those who make them, and all who trust them
  become like them: fused atmosphere.

¹⁹ Praise the LORD, O Israelites.
  Praise him, O Aaronites.
²⁰ Praise the LORD, each of you Levites.
  Praise him, all who fear him aright.[215]
²¹ Praise the LORD from the city of Zion.
  Let praise to him be outpoured.
Praise him who lives in Jerusalem.
  HALLELU-YAH, PRAISE THE LORD.

---

[212] This line's information is implied from "wiping them out" but it is not specifically repeated in the Hebrew text.

[213] The more literal expression of v 17b is "there is no breath in their mouth."

[214] This line is implied in the overall image but is not in the literal Hebrew text.

[215] Fearing him aright is to revere him and it includes a respectful fear of his power and authority over our lives.

Psalm 136

¹ Give thanks to the LORD
>   because he is good, ...
>> FOR HIS LOVE IS STEADFAST,
>> FOREVER IT WILL LAST.[216]

²⁻³ Give thanks to the God above all gods,
>   the Lord above all lords, ...
>> FOR HIS LOVE IS STEADFAST,
>> FOREVER IT WILL LAST.

⁴⁻⁶ Give thanks to the unique, wonder-working God,
>   who made the heavens with skill,
who spread out the dry ground
>   on the seas by his will, ...
>> FOR HIS LOVE IS STEADFAST,
>> FOREVER IT WILL LAST.

⁷⁻⁹ Give thanks to him
>   who made each great light:
the sun to rule day,
>   the moon and stars night, ...
>> FOR HIS LOVE IS STEADFAST,
>> FOREVER IT WILL LAST.

¹⁰⁻¹² Give thanks to him
>   who struck down Egypt's firstborn
>> with a strong hand,
>   who brought out Israel with power
>> to a promised land, ...[217]
>>> FOR HIS LOVE IS STEADFAST,
>>> FOREVER IT WILL LAST.

---

[216] The 26 refrains of the original text "for his love is steadfast, forever it will last" have been reduced to 9 in this poetic version. This is a matter of style in English. You still can still feel the emphasis of the refrain with 9 repetitions.
[217] The expression "**promised land**" is only clearly mentioned in Hebrews 11:9, and not specifically in the Hebrew text, but the concept is very clearly emphasized throughout the Hebrew Scriptures.

¹³ Give thanks to him
　　　who divided the Red Sea in two,
　　　¹⁴ and brought his people through,
　　　¹⁵ but Pharaoh and his army, slew.²¹⁸
　　　　　¹⁶ And even in the desert,
　　　he led his people through, ...
　　　　　　FOR HIS LOVE IS STEADFAST,
　　　　　　FOREVER IT WILL LAST.

¹⁷⁻¹⁸ Give thanks to him
　　　who killed famous kings:
　　　　　　¹⁹ Sihon the Amorite
　　　　　　²⁰ and Og the Bashanite,
　　　　　　　　²¹ and gave their land away,
　　　　　　　　　　²² to Israel his servant
　　　　　　　to inherit on that day, ...
　　　　　　　　　FOR HIS LOVE IS STEADFAST,
　　　　　　　　　FOREVER IT WILL LAST.

²³ Give thanks to him
　　　who remembered us
　　　　　　when we were brought low,
　　²⁴⁻²⁵ who gives food to each creature
　　　　　and freed us from each foe, ...
　　　　　　　FOR HIS LOVE IS STEADFAST,
　　　　　　　FOREVER IT WILL LAST.

²⁶ Give thanks to the God who dwells in heaven.
　　　YES, HIS LOVE IS STEADFAST,
　　　FOREVER IT WILL LAST.

---

²¹⁸ The Hebrew text indicates that they were slain in the sea. This information is left implicit in the text.

Psalm 137

[1] There at the rivers of Babylon,
when we thought about Jerusalem,
    we hung our heads and cried.
[2] On the willows there, we hung up our harps,
[3] when our captors tortured us with barbs.
    We felt like we had died.[219]
They asked for joyful songs, short or long.[220]
"Hey, sing for us a Zion song!"
    they made as a demand.
[4] But how can we strike up singing,
the LORD's choruses ringing
    in a foreign land?

[5] Jerusalem, if I forget you,
    may my hand-strum skills undo.[221]
[6] May my tongue be numb so I can't sing,
    if I don't remember you.
If I don't view you as my greatest joy,
    then I would be untrue.[222]

[7] Remember, LORD, what those Edomites said,
    when Jerusalem was crushed that day.
"Raze it down, raze it all down!" they yelled.
    "Destroy them, come what may!"
[8] O Babylon, destined for doom and downfall,
    as you have treated us,
        favored are all
            who repay you.
[9] Favored are those
    who grab your babies,
        and to the sharp rocks go, ...
        and break them in two.

---

[219] This line is implied but not part of the Hebrew text.

[220] "Short or long" is not part of the Hebrew text.

[221] Lit. "may my right hand forget" probably means "may I forget how to play the harp."

[222] This line is implied but not part of the Hebrew text.

Psalm 138

Written by David.

1 I'll thank you, LORD, with all my being,
　　　　before angels I'll sing your praise.
2 I'll worship toward your holy temple.
　　　　Your name I'll lift high always.
I'll praise you for your faithfulness,
　　　　and for your loyal love,
for you've raised up your name and word
　　　　higher than the sky above.223
　　　　3 The day I called you answered my prayer.
　　　　You've strengthened me by your care.

4 All earthly kings will thank you, LORD,
　　　　for they've heard the words you state.
5 They'll sing about your ways, O LORD,
　　　　because your glory is great.
6 You're high, yet you see the lowly.
　　　　The proud are far from your gate.

7 I live with troubles all around,
　　　　but you save and set me free.
You defend me from my foes' anger.
　　　　By your might you'll rescue me.

8 I'm sure LORD, you'll bring me justice.
　　　　Your great love is always there.
You've made me with your skillful hands.
　　　　Don't discard me from your care.

Psalm 139

For the music director. A psalm written by David.

1 You've plumbed the depths of my heart, O LORD,
　　　　and you know all about me.
2 If I sit down or stand up – you know it.
　　　　My thoughts from afar you see.

---

223 Lit. "You've made all your name great over your word." Difficult to interpret.
"For you have exalted above everything your name and your word" (RSV).

3 If I walk about or lie down,
      you observe each path I take.
All of my ways you know full well,
      whether sleeping or awake.[224]
4 Before I even speak a word, LORD,
      you know it fully, you see.
5 You're behind me, in front, all around.
      Your blessing is upon me.
6 It transcends me, upends me, ... your knowledge
      reaches far beyond me.

7 Where can I flee from your Spirit?
      Your presence is everywhere.
8 If I rise to heaven, descend to the grave,
      each place I go, you're there.
9 If I rise on dawn's wings or could live
      on the far ends of the sea,
10 even there you're with me and hold me up,
      and firmly you would guide me.
11 If I were to say: "Hide me!" to darkness,
      or to light around me: "Be night!"
12 Even in this, the darkness itself
      cannot hide from your sight.
For you God, you see through the darkness.
      Darkness to you is as light.

13-14 You fashioned the inward parts of me.
      I'm a beautiful creation!
You sculpted me inside my mother.
      What a wondrous formation!
I praise you for your stunning works.
      I'm awestruck with elation!
15 My flesh and bones weren't hidden from you
      in the depths of my mother's womb.
In this dark and secret chamber
      I was woven on your loom.

---

[224] Though true, this line is not in the Hebrew text. It is added for rhyme.

¹⁶ Even as an amorphous fetus,
      I was wholly in your view.
My fore-ordained days you wrote them down.
      You know me through and through.
¹⁷ How amazing and precious, O God,
      are your endless thoughts toward me.
¹⁸ They're more than all the grains of sand,
      countless, like infinity.
When I awake in the morning,
      you still abide with me.

¹⁹⁻²⁰ O God, your foes blaspheme your name.
      Each one's your enemy.
Destroy them, those cold-blooded killers!
      You wicked! Depart from me!
²¹⁻²² Should not my thoughts on your foes be like this?
      Your enemy, my enemy!
Should not I hate those who war with you?
      Yes, to the nth degree!
²³Look deep, O God, and test me fully.
      Probe my mind and heart all my days.
²⁴Show me each thing that offends you.
      Guide me in your timeless ways.

Psalm 140
                For the music director. A psalm written by David.
¹ Deliver me, LORD, from evil people,
      from beasts who strike brutally.
² Yes, these are those who plot evil schemes,
      and wage war constantly.
³ They have tongues like venomous vipers,
      and speak contemptuously.   *Pause and reflect*

⁴⁻⁵ Protect me, LORD, **from the wicked's power.**
      The violent rise against me.
These prideful people try to trip me up,
      their perilous plots you see.

They lay out their traps along my path,
      and wait with nets to catch me.   *Pause and reflect*

6-7 O Yahweh, my Lord, my Savior and God,
      I need your help, hear my cry.
You keep me safe in all my battles.
    `   You're my support and supply.[225]
8 O Lord, **don't give the wicked** their desires.
      Defeat them in schemes they try.   *Pause and reflect*

9 When leaders of foes around me rise up,
      may they reap what their lips have sown.
10 May they be judged with fiery coals,
      and into the fire be thrown.
May they be flung into muddy pits,
      never again to stand.
11 May misfortune hunt down the violent,
      may cruel liars fail in the land.

12 LORD, I know you'll be just to the needy,
      and defend the rights of the poor.
13 Surely the just and godly will thank you,
      and live with you evermore.[226]

Psalm 141

A psalm written by David.

1 Hear my prayer, LORD, come quickly to help.
      Unto you I lift up my cries.
2 Accept this prayer as an offering,
      like incense to you may it rise.
As I raise my hands to you, receive it as
      an evening sacrifice.

---

[225] This line gives implied details of how God provides for the psalmist.
[226] The Hebrew text is more ambiguous "living in your presence," but it is possibly implied that this will last forever, and this is taught elsewhere in Scripture.

3-4 Let my thoughts not drift to what's evil,
  or practice wicked acts.
Let me not join with doers of wrong,
  or partake of their tempting snacks.227
Set a guard at the door of my mouth, LORD.
  Watch over how I react.

5 If a godly man corrects me,
  that's a kindness instead!
If he rebukes me, I'll accept it,
  that's lotion on my head!
But my prayer will condemn the wicked,
  for evil acts they've spread.
6 When their leaders are hurled off high cliffs,
  people will say: "Your words were true.
7 Like broken ground when the earth is plowed,
  at Death's door228 our bones are strewn."

8 Yahweh, my Lord, on you I fix my gaze.
  I seek shelter in you.
Don't let me be turned over to them.
  Don't let them run me through.229
9 Wrongdoers set traps and snares for me.
  Protect me from what they do.
10 Make them fall into their own traps,
  while I pass safely through.

---

227 This is used in a figurative sense. Compare, "Don't let me even taste the good things they offer" (CEV).

228 Hebrew: "the mouth of *Sheol*." Death's door is a metaphor for the grave to represent the personification of "*Sheol*'s mouth." The interpretation for vv 6-7 is very difficult. Note carefully the quotes here.

229 These two lines (8cd) are an expansion of the more literal "do not lay bare my life" which means "Don't let me die" (NCV).

Psalm 142

A contemplative song by David. A prayer written when he was in a cave.

1 I pray to you, LORD, I plead for favor.
> Hear my voice as I cry out.
2 I pour out to you all my troubles
> which are knocking me about.

3 When I grow weak and feel overwhelmed,
> it's you who leads me ahead.
My foes have hidden an ambush for me
> in the very path I tread.
4 When I look for help, none is near.
> No one's tends to my affairs.
There's no place of refuge to run to,
> and no one around me cares.
5 I cry out to you, LORD, my shelter,
> I live as one of your heirs.

6 Listen for I'm sunk down in sorrow.
> Hear now my urgent cry!
Save from those who chase after me,
> for they are stronger than I.
7 Deliver me so I can thank you.
> From this prison set me free.
Then the godly will rush to my side,
> for you've been good to me.

Psalm 143

A psalm written by David.

1 Hear my prayer LORD, for you are faithful.
> Come help me for you do what's right.
2 Don't put your servant on trial.
> No one is just in your sight.

3 My enemies chased me to kill me.
> They've knocked me down hard to the ground.
They've caused me to live in dark places,
> like dead ones no longer around.

4 My hope fades and I'm grieved in spirit.
     I'm numb inside with great fear.
5 I remember past times, and what you've done.
     I reflect on your works so clear.
6 I'm like a dry desert: I thirst for you.
     I lift hands and pray you'll come near. *Pause and reflect*

7 Respond now, O LORD, I'm losing all hope.
     Don't turn away from me.
Or I'll be like those who plunge to the Pit,
     until they cease to be.
8 Let me hear each morning of your great love,
     for I'm fully trusting in you.
Reveal to me the road I should take.
     My life's yours in all I do.

9-10 I seek to please you. You are my God.
     In all of your ways, please teach me.
Deliver me from my foes, O LORD.
     Give me help for to you I flee.[230]
Move me, Good Spirit, to a smooth place.
     May you to safety lead me.

11 For the sake of your name, LORD,
     protect fully my life.
Because you are righteous,
     bring me out of this strife.
12 Because of your great love,
     wipe out those who oppose.
Because I'm your servant,
     destroy all my foes.

---

[230] The rendering "I flee" is based on the Septuagint's reading of the Hebrew text and on one Hebrew manuscript. The Hebrew text reads "to you" as in "I go to you for protection." See the NET Bible footnote for v 9.

Psalm 144

Written by David.

1 May you be praised, O LORD, my Rock.
  You've trained me for war to fight.
2 You are my loving God and Savior,
    my Fortress and my Might.
You hide me, shield me, and cause the nations
    to bow to my oversight.

3 LORD, why do you notice us mortals?
    Or why do you even care?
4 Our days, they pass like a shadow.
  We're like a puff of air.
5 O LORD, descend, bend down the skies,
    touch the mountains and pour out smoke.
6 Flash lightning and arrows, fluster my foes.
    Smite them with a deadly stroke.
7 Stretch down from above, pull me from deep seas.
    Save from rivals who pulverize,
8 WHO TAKE SOLEMN OATHS, THEN BREAK THEM,
    AND SPEAK NOTHING BUT LIES.

9 I'll sing to you a triumph song, O God,
    while playing my harp to you.[231]
10 You strengthen kings to win, and David,
    you save him in war and coup.
11 Rescue me from enemy strongholds,
    from rivals who pulverize,
WHO TAKE SOLEMN OATHS, THEN BREAK THEM,
    AND SPEAK NOTHING BUT LIES.

12 May our young sons be robust plants,
    our daughters, carved columns of gold,
        adorning the palace like treasure.

---

[231] Lit. "new song," see the footnote for Ps 96:1-2. Note how Ps 144 is a military context, implying a song of victory or triumph here. The instrument here was probably a ten-stringed instrument.

13 May crops fill our barns with fruitful advance,
      our flocks gain a thousandfold,
           multiplying beyond measure.
14 May our cattle produce abundantly,
      without loss or miscarriage.
May outcries disappear in our streets,
      and cries from being ravaged.

15 Favored are those for whom this is true,
whose God is the LORD in all they do!

Psalm 145

A psalm of praise written by David.

א (Aleph)   1 I'll praise your name, my God and King.
                  I'll magnify you always.

ב (Beth)   2 Forever I'll honor your name.
                  I'll praise you all my days.

ג (Gimel)   3 Great is the LORD. Who can grasp how much so?
                  He is worthy of highest praise.

ד (Daleth)   4 One generation will praise to the next,
                  your mighty works and ways.

ה (He)   5 I will declare your majestic splendor.
                  On your wonders I'll contemplate.

ו (Waw)   6 All will speak of your marvelous acts.
                  Your greatness I'll propagate.

ז (Zayin)   7 All will shout of your justice with joy.
                  Your goodness they'll celebrate.

ח (Heth)   8 The LORD is full of grace and compassion,
                  loyal in love, slow to rage.

ט (Teth)   9 To all he is good and shows tenderness,
                  to all that he has made.

י (Yodh)   10 All your works give you thanks, O LORD,
                  your faithful ones give you praise.

כ (Kaph)   11 They speak of your kingdom's glory,
                  and of your powerful ways.

ל **(Lamedh)** [12] Then the world will know of your great deeds,
and the splendor of your reign.
מ **(Mem)** [13] Your kingdom is an eternal kingdom,
a never-ending domain.

נ **(Nun)** The LORD is faithful in each thing he does,
true to each promise expressed.[232]
ס **(Samekh)** [14] The LORD supports all who are falling,
and upholds all the oppressed.
ע **(Ayin)** [15] All eyes look to you and at the right time,
their needed food you give.
פ **(Pe)** [16] You give so freely and satisfy
the desires of all who live.
צ **(Tsadhe)** [17] In all his works the LORD is faithful.
In his ways, he's just in them all.
ק **(Qoph)** [18] He's near to all who cry out to him,
to each who sincerely call.
ר **(Resh)** [19] To all who fear him he grants their desires.
He hears their help-cry and saves.
שׂ/שׁ **(Sin/Shin)** [20] The LORD will protect all who love him,
but send the wicked to graves.[233]

ת **(Taw)** [21] I'll praise the LORD in each endeavor.
May all who live praise his holy name.
To him be praise forever.

Psalm 146
[1] HALLELU-YAH, PRAISE THE LORD.
I'll praise him with my whole being.
[2] I'll sing praise to God as long as I live,
as long as I keep on breathing.

---

[232] These two lines of the nun verse are not found in most Hebrew manuscripts of
the Masoretic text but are found in the Dead Sea Scrolls, Septuagint, Syriac and
one Hebrew manuscript.
[233] Lit. "but all the wicked he will destroy."

3 Don't put your trust in a person.
       Even great leaders can't save you.
4 When they perish and return to the ground,
       then their plans will perish too.
5-6 Those who are truly favored
       will find help in Jacob's God,
the Maker of earth, sky, and sea —
       of all things near and abroad.
It's he who's eternally faithful.
       Their trust's in the LORD their God.

7-8 The LORD gives food to the hungry,
       grants justice to the oppressed.
He gives sight to those who are blind,
       frees captives who are suppressed.
The LORD loves those who do what is right,
       and raises up those bowed down.
9 He cares for strangers, widows, and orphans,
       but throws wicked ones to the ground.[234]

10 O Zion, your LORD God rules forever.
       Let praise to him be outpoured.
He will reign through all generations.
       HALLELU-YAH, PRAISE THE LORD.

Psalm 147

1 HALLELU-YAH, PRAISE THE LORD.
Let praise to him be outpoured.

It is good and pleasant to praise our God.
       To praise him is so right.
2-3 The LORD's rebuilding Jerusalem
       with those outcast from his sight.[235]

---

[234] Lit. "bends the ways of the wicked" meaning their plans are frustrated or defeated by God.

[235] Most scholars believe that this psalm is post-exilic because of the wording here which naturally fits into the idea of the "exile."

He heals broken hearts in Israel,
    and binds up their wounds tight.

4 He calculates the number of stars,
    and gives each a name all around.
5 He has all power and greatness,
    his knowledge knows no bounds.
6 The LORD lifts up all the oppressed,
    the wicked he throws to the ground.

7 Sing praises to our God with the harp.
    Sing thanks to the LORD, glorify.
8 He sends clouds to bring earth its rain.
    He fills hills with grass by and by.
9 He gives all the beasts their food,
    and feeds young birds when they cry.

10-11 Does the LORD rejoice at a horse's strength?
    Or a strong man's legs does he speak of?
No, he's pleased with those who revere him,
    who trust in his loyal love.

12 Glorify the LORD, O Jerusalem.
    Give praise to your God anew.
13 For he fortifies your city gates,
    and blesses the children in you.
14 He fills you full with the finest wheat,
    and secures your borders too.

15 He sends forth his message on earth.
    How quickly his word flies.
16 He scatters snow like a blanket of wool.
    He spreads frost – like ashes it lies.
17 He hurls his hail like icy stones.
    Who can endure his cold blows?
18 He sends forth his word and everything melts.
    He blows breezes and each stream flows.

¹⁹⁻²⁰ His laws he's not shown to other nations,²³⁶
>   but to Israel he commands
his judgments and regulations,
>   his words and his demands.

Let praise to him be outpoured.
HALLELU-YAH, PRAISE THE LORD.

Psalm 148
¹ HALLELU-YAH, PRAISE THE LORD.
Let praise to him be outpoured.

Praise the LORD from heaven,
>   praise him from a great height.
² Praise him, you his angels,
>   praise him, you armies of might.²³⁷
³ Praise him sun, praise him moon,
>   and you bright stars likewise.
⁴ Praise him, you highest heaven,
>   and waters above the skies.

⁵ He himself ordered that they be created.
>   Let them lift the LORD's name in praise.
⁶ He made an irrevocable law
>   that they be established always.

⁷ Praise the LORD, you on the earth,
>   you sea monsters, you ocean deep.
⁸ Lightning and hail – clouds, snow, and gale,
>   his word you hear and keep.
⁹⁻¹⁰ Mountains, hills, wild and tame beasts,
>   reptiles, birds, fruit trees and cedars.

---

²³⁶ "Has not shown his laws to other nations" follows the Septuagint text and is found in a Dead Sea Scroll Hebrew text. The Masoretic Text has "they do not know his laws."

²³⁷ This probably refers to divine spiritual beings in heaven.

¹¹⁻¹² Young men and women, old and young alike,
   nations, kings, rulers and leaders.

¹³ Let them all praise the name of the LORD,
   for his name alone is extolled.
His splendor transcends earth and sky.
   It's a wonder to behold.²³⁸
¹⁴ He protects and honors his people.²³⁹
   He has made them strong.
He watches over faithful Israel,
   for to him they belong.

Let praise to him be outpoured.
HALLELU-YAH, PRAISE THE LORD.

Psalm 149
¹ HALLELU-YAH, PRAISE THE LORD.
Let praise to him be outpoured.
   Sing to him a victory song.²⁴⁰
   Sing his praise, O faithful throng,
   in the assembly strong.

² Let Israel celebrate their maker.
   Let Zion rejoice in their King!
³ Let them praise his name with music and dance.
   With hand drum and harp, let them sing.
⁴ The LORD saves and beautifies the humble.
   In his people he takes delight.
⁵ Let the faithful exult in God's glory,
   and sing for joy through the night.

⁶ May God's high praises be on their lips,
   with two-edged swords in their hands,

---

²³⁸ This implied line is not in the Hebrew text.
²³⁹ Literally here, "he has raised up a horn for his people." The horn symbolizes strength or protection or both.
²⁴⁰ Lit. "new song," probably means a "song of victory" here. See note on Ps 96:1.

7 to bring judgment on the peoples,
    and vengeance on the lands,

8 to bind kings and rulers with shackles,
    pictures of victory runs,
9 to bring on them the judgment decreed,
    an honor for God's faithful ones.

Let praise to him be outpoured.
HALLELU-YAH, PRAISE THE LORD!

Psalm 150

1HALLELU-YAH, PRAISE THE LORD.
Let all things praise the LORD.

Praise God in the heights of heaven.
    Praise him in the holy place.
2Praise him for his powerful deeds.
    Praise him who's supremely great.
3 Praise him with trumpet blasts.
    Praise him with harps and lutes.241
4 Praise him with hand drum and dance.
    Praise him with strings and flutes.
        5 Let cymbals resound, their voices raise.
        With crashing noise, let percussion praise.

        6May each who breathes, each living thing,
        unto the LORD let praises ring,

Let all things praise the LORD.
HALLELU-YAH, PRAISE THE LORD.

---

241 Although lutes are medieval instruments, some scholars believe that the *kinnor* may have looked like a lute with multiple strings and a round back. So, the translation captures an image of what would be more accurately called a "lute-like instrument." Interestingly many translations like ESV, CSB, and NRSV choose "lute" here. The other instrument in the verse *nevel* may have been a framed harp. However, there is much scholarly debate as to how to translate *kinnor* and *nevel*.

www.ingramcontent.com/pod-product-compliance
Lightning Source LLC
Chambersburg PA
CBHW030924090426
42737CB00007B/312

www.ingramcontent.com/pod-product-compliance
Lightning Source LLC
Chambersburg PA
CBHW030924090426
42737CB00007B/312